BUDDY STALL'S
LOUISIANA POTPOURRI

BUDDY STALL'S
LOUISIANA POTPOURRI

By Gaspar J. ("Buddy") Stall

PELICAN PUBLISHING COMPANY
Gretna 1991

Library of Congress Catalog Card Number: 91-76491

ISBN: 0-88289-913-9

Manufactured in the United States of America

Published by Pelican Publishing Company, Inc.
1101 Monroe Street, Gretna, Louisiana 70053

Dedicated to:

My mother, called by her friends T. T.
(Theresa Trapani-Stall);

My father, known by his many friends as the Iron Man;

And my brother, who had enough nicknames
to fill this page,
but always called by me, Brother.

Acknowledgements

Special thanks to Roxanne Ryan, Clyde Morrison, Lane Casteix, Kitty Garvey, Yvette Ponthier, Elizabeth Ann Carter, Irvin Bergeron, Carol and Jim Rohde, Marietta and Richard Herr, Joe d'Aquin, Judge Dick Garvey, as well as to the following people: Collin Hamer and the entire staff of the Louisiana Division of the New Orleans Public Library, Pamela Arceneaux and the entire staff of the Historic New Orleans Collection, Bob Dennie of Louisiana Wildlife and Fisheries Commission and Bob Breck of Channel 8 Television.

CONTENTS

CHAPTER 1

DISCOVERY

FIRST LIQUID

THEN LAND

FINALLY MAN

DISCOVERY OF LOUISIANA

DISCOVERY OF THE MOUTH OF THE
MISSISSIPPI RIVER

BUDDY STALL'S LOUISIANA POTPOURRI

CHAPTER 1

LIQUID

Between 64 and 250 million years ago, when dinosaurs roamed the earth, the present land area of Louisiana was under the ocean. The receding water level reached mid-state

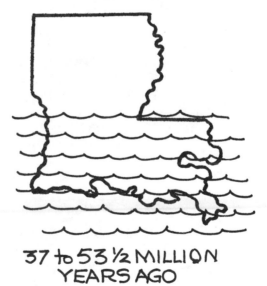

37 to 53 ½ MILLION YEARS AGO

37 to 53.5 million years ago. All except the most southern part of the state was formed about 1.8 million years ago.

It is not an easy task to visualize giant water snakes 45 feet long swimming over what is now Louisiana. Swimming along

with the monstrous snakes were fish of every size and variety, including massive sharks and giant whales that stretched out to 60 feet. Today, the only proof that these creatures existed in this area are fossils collected by paleontologists, archaeologists, geologists and anthropologists who preserved them in their private collections or museums. One such find of a giant whale

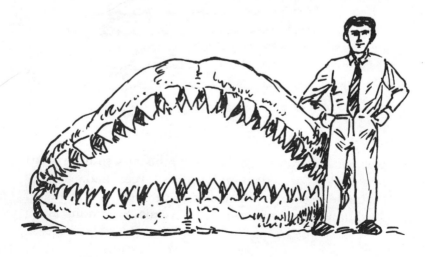

was made at Montgomery Landing, about 30 miles south of
Alexandria. It included a skull four feet long and the front
third of its skeleton. The fossils of giant sharks proved they
were as described, massive. One of the shark jaws measured a
phenomenal eight feet. This proves they were certainly as big
as the great white whales, maybe even bigger.

One of the best local displays of the remains of these
creatures can be viewed at the Museum of Natural Science on
the Louisiana State University campus in Baton Rouge.

One million years ago, after the waters had receded and
glaciers covered much of North America, Louisiana became a
forest of spruce trees. Enormous mastodons, resembling giant

long-tusk elephants , roamed through our state. Saber tooth
tigers and herds of bison (buffalo) were commonplace. A
good example of the remains of a mastodon was found just
north of Baton Rouge, at what is today Clifford Plantation on
Tunica Bayou. Its remains are also on display at LSU's Museum
of Natural Science. Additional mastodon fossils were taken
from Cooper Plantation on Bayou Manchac in Ascension
Parish and from Percy Plantation on Bayou Sara in West
Feliciana Parish.

There has been much debate over why the mastodons and

tigers died out. Two possible explanations are foremost; the animals were hunted to extinction, or the changing climate and retreating glaciers adversely affected the animals.

The buffalo must have been the heartiest as well as the most numerous of the animals, for they survived the longest. The first reported sighting of them was by Pere Jacques Marquette on an expedition in 1673. He wrote in his journal that the wild cattle (bison) roamed everywhere in large herds. In 1699, when Sieur Jean Baptiste Lemoine de Bienville and his party camped out at what was later to become the city of New Orleans, he recorded in his journal that they had killed a buffalo and ate it for dinner. That was the first reported meal found by the author to be eaten in the state of Louisiana.

The last reported buffalo killed in Louisiana came in 1803 when one was shot along the Ouachita River near Monroe.

LAND

Twenty thousand years before the time of Christ, an era known as the Ice Age, glaciers covered large portions of the world. In North America, ice extended as far south as southern Illinois (see map, page 18). Over the thousands of years that the ice melted, the run-off sought the lowest level of land, cutting a channel and forming a great river in the central part of the continent. This body of water is known today as the mighty Mississippi River.

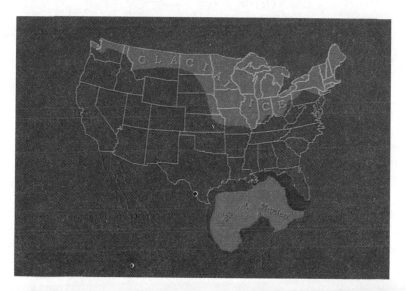

Each year, top soil of 33 states, from as far west as Montana, and from New York to the east, is deposited into the bowels of the great river. Over the centuries, at its very end, the river moved back and forth like a snake depositing the silt it carried as it moved farther and farther south. For hundreds of years, it moved from east to west and back again many, many times. The restless river emptied to the east as far as present-day Pascagoula, Mississippi, and to the west as far as what is now known as the city of Lafayette. Since it was the top soil of thirty-three states and two provinces of Canada that built part of the

state of Louisiana, Louisianians naturally consider their state to be the best of all the rest. Because of this phenomenon, Louisiana, especially the delta portions, are considered the world's most fertile and most productive area to be found on the face of the earth.

It has been jokingly pointed out that every time they flush a commode in Chicago, they do so to help Louisiana. Louisianians have built levees to protect themselves from such things.

LAST FOUR LOUISIANA DELTAS
AND WHEN THEY WERE FORMED

TECHE DELTA: 2500 B.C.

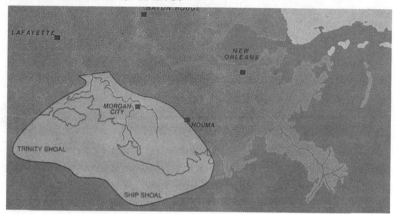

At approximately the same time civilization gave birth to the pyramids and great sphinxes in Egypt, the Teche Delta was being formed. It is the oldest lobe of the Mississippi Delta and began building in about 5000 B.C., or, if you prefer, approximately 7000 years ago. The Teche Delta reached its peak around 2500 B.C.

The Mississippi River flowed into the Teche area for about 2500 years. After that, it overflowed its bank and moved eastward where it began creating the next delta.

ST. BERNARD DELTA: 1000 B.C.

When the very first Olympic games were held, and Rome was being built, the birth of the St. Bernard Delta began. It was at this time the Chandeleur Islands in the Gulf of Mexico were born, along with what is now the city of New Orleans. Once the Mississippi River began flowing into the St. Bernard area, the earlier Teche Delta began to compact, subside and wash away. Portions of the original Teche gradually disappeared beneath the surface of the Gulf.

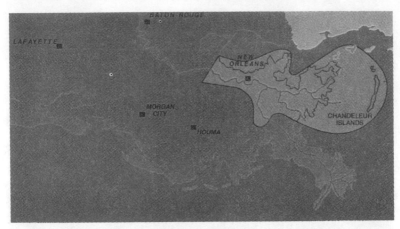

After about 1500 years, the Mississippi abandoned its course in St. Bernard, cutting off the nurturing sediment supply. Just as the original Teche Delta changed in size, the same occurred in the St. Bernard Delta. The compacting, subsidence and wash away is evident by the fact the St. Bernard Delta, when built, had land all the way to the present day Chandeleur Islands (see drawing page 49).

The Mississippi River, like a slithering snake, moved again to the west. She was now ready to build the next delta.

LAFOURCHE DELTA: 1300 A.D.

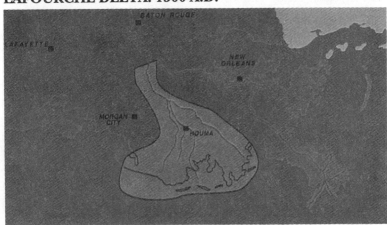

As the Lafourche Delta was being formed, the Renaissance was taking place in Italy and fire arms were invented. As the river had done on numerous occasions, after the Lafourche Delta was built, she was ready for her next and last move. The last delta is referred to as the Modern Delta.

MODERN DELTA

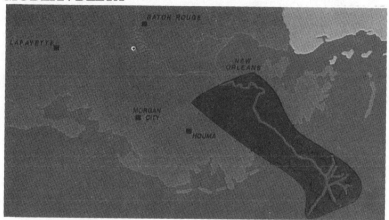

The Modern Delta, or, as some refer to it, the Bird Foot Delta, at 700 years old, is relatively new. It was born at the same time in history that playing cards were invented in France. Those who make their homes in the low deltas take a chance against rising waters, just as those who play cards take a risk of losing their money.

LAST SILT DEPOSITS BEFORE LEVEES

If it were not for man building levees to protect the people living adjacent to the river from flooding, the mighty Mississippi River would certainly change its course again. It is also interesting to surmise what the shape of Louisiana would be now had man not interfered by harnessing the river with levees.

As the adage goes, for every action there is certain to be a reaction. Because man has harnessed the river, it is no longer

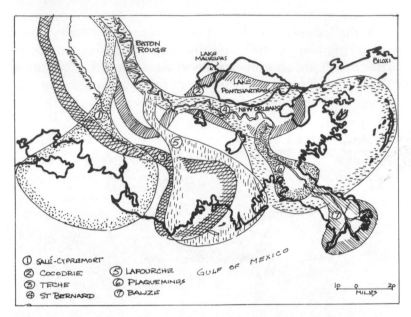

① SALÉ-CYPREMORT
② COCODRIE   ⑤ LAFOURCHE
③ TECHE   ⑥ PLAQUEMINES
④ ST BERNARD   ⑦ BALIZE

GULF OF MEXICO

MILES

allowed to deposit sediment to continue to build land mass. This has certainly created a problem that is monumental in scope. The problem is called coastal erosion.

By tampering with nature, man must now pay the consequences. But wait a minute — are we sure the river would have changed its course again if we had left it alone? Experts say you can bet your sweet bippy, probably by way of the Atchafalaya basin. Since man has tampered with nature, the consequences we are suffering and will continue to suffer will require drastic actions, costing not millions but billions of dollars. Louisiana is losing 30 to 40 square miles (one acre every ten minutes) of nutrient-rich coastal wetlands every year. "What's the big deal?" you say. "It's only marshland." Lets put it in dollars and cents so that we can see just how the situation drastically affects the economy and recreation.

The commercial fish and shellfish harvest is valued at 680 million dollars annually. This represents about forty percent of the nation's supply. This one industry alone employs 40 thousand Louisianians. In the fur industry, two million pelts a year are processed. Louisiana is the number one producer of furs in North America. The state produces more furs than the next three largest fur producing states combined. The economic dollar value is 25 million. Louisiana's crawfish crop is valued at 12.1 million. Alligator hides bring in 2.6 million dollars. The alligator meat adds additional revenue. Water fowl hunting is valued at 58 million annually. Hunting, fishing and other water related recreation dollars exceed 337 million dollars annually. Twenty-seven percent of the state's population participate in using this area of recreation.

If the marshes continue to wash away, billions of dollars of business in Louisiana will wash away with it. Not only will Louisiana citizens suffer both economically and recreationally, people all over the North American continent will also be affected. The reason, Louisiana marsh lands serve as the habitat for sixty-six percent of the nation's migrating water fowl. Where these birds will go if Louisiana marsh lands are lost is a mystery.

COASTAL EROSION PROJECTION

If coastal erosion is left unchecked, the map below is a prediction of what could be the potential outcome by 2040 A.D.

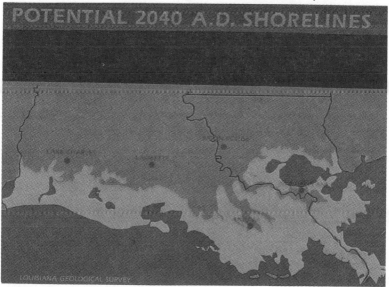

TONGUE IN CHEEK HUMOR

To end on a humorous note of a highly serious situation, see the cartoon below.

MAN

In 1492, when Christopher Columbus landed on the shores of North America, believing he had reached India, he mistakenly called the natives Indians. Although the North American natives and inhabitants of India both have dark brown skin and straight black hair, the similarities of the two races end there. Unfortunately, the error made by Columbus has filtered down through generations and no doubt will exist until the end of time.

Where did those early inhabitants in Louisiana come from, and how long have they occupied this area? As is true so often in history, there are conflicting beliefs as to where they came from and only a guesstimate as to when they arrived. The reason: the American Indians had no knowledge of the written word. Therefore, conflicting opinions will certainly be left, as is the norm, in the minds of the archaeologists. Who knows, with some luck the truth will ultimately be learned.

The closest estimate as to when they first arrived in present day Louisiana is 12,000 years ago, possibly even earlier. To be sure, the inhabitants were living in Louisiana long, long before Christopher Columbus left Spain.

As to where they came from, there are two schools of thought.

FIRST:

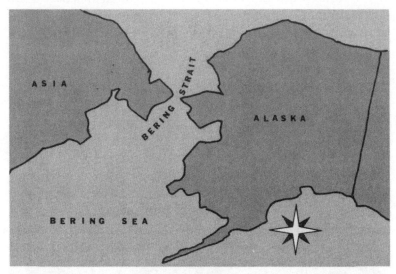

A small band of men, about 50,000 B.C., wandered from the cold lands of northeastern Asia across the Bering Strait into what is now Alaska. Because of the vast amount of water which was then locked in Ice Age glaciers, the sea level was considerably lower than it is today. What is now the Bering Strait was then a land bridge between the present-day Soviet Union and Alaska.

Those scholars who subscribe to this theory as to where the first Louisiana inhabitants came from are quick to point out the fact that early arrivals used bolas for hunting. The bola is made of rocks with holes or grooves bored in them and tied together with strips of rawhide or vine. Bolas were used mainly to hunt water fowl, a method long used by Eskimos in the frozen land of the north. They are also quick to point out that evidence exists that shows the first inhabitants used spears to hunt with (bows and arrows were not used until sometime between 950 and 1300 A.D.). The Indians combined the spear (harpoon) with the atlatl (spear thrower). This method of throwing the spear, also used by the Eskimos, proved to be more effective in hunting.

The atlatl, or spear thrower

The atlatl is simply a stick with a notch at one end to which the butt end of the spear is hooked, so that when the atlatl, which is held at the other end by the throwing hand, is slung forward the spear can be sent farther and harder than it could be if thrown only with an unaided arm.

The spear was eventually copied and used by white men for hunting whales.

Those early Arctic adventurers, some called the real discoverers of America, moved steadily down the coast and throughout the interior of the rich New World. By 10,000 B.C., they had reached the southern tip of South America.

SECOND:

A second possibility did not come to light until this century. Almost all traces of civilization before the time of the alphabet are found through archaeological diggings. In 1955, an archaeologist with a trained eye made a most unusual discovery of a civilization with a population of 5,000 at its peak. He found it not through the normal digging but while flying 10,000 feet above the earth. What he saw was a geometrically perfect series of concentric circles on the land. Having studied and previously visited such sites, he instantly knew this was the remains of a unique Indian village. The area he discovered from the air is located on Bayou Macon in West Carroll Parish.

The second theory as to where the Indians came from is based on the fact that identical designs, constructions, and

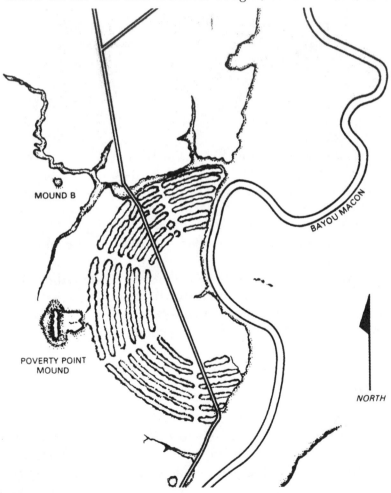

artifacts like those in north Louisiana, estimated to be 3,000 years old, are also located in Japan and Ecuador. Testing of the sights in Japan and Ecuador shows them both to be around 6,000 B.C. Therefore, it is believed by many serious scholars that the lower Mississippi Valley was inhabited by immigrants from a very distant culture. It is highly possible that long before man learned to record his adventures, wave after wave of hardy Japanese fishermen, in incredibly fragile craft, island hopped their way across the wide Pacific Ocean and landed somewhere on the coast of present-day Ecuador. After establishing a community in Ecuador, it is believed they made their way across the Gulf of Mexico, a relatively easy task compared to crossing the Pacific Ocean. Upon reaching North America, they made their way up the waterways, settling in many areas, among them a wooded site on Bayou Macon in Louisiana's West Carroll Parish. The area today is known as Poverty Point. (Drawing of Poverty Point, page 28)

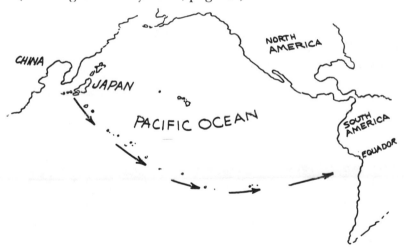

These prehistoric Indians built their city on six six-foot high concentric circles of earth. Each ridge is approximately 150 feet wide and 6 feet high, with the outside circle 3/4 of a mile in diameter. Two ceremonial mounds were raised, the largest as high as a seven-story building, with the shape of a bird in flight on the very top. The amount of dirt moved by hand in these earthworks staggers the imagination. The living circle alone contains thirty-five times the cubic content of the great pyramid of Cheops in Egypt.

Both theories as to where the original inhabitants came from have merit. Who knows, maybe the Japanese headed north from the Gulf of Mexico and the Asians started in Alaska and migrated south.

One thing is for sure, the prehistoric Indians were 180 degrees different from the Indians we have come to know through current books and movies. The Indians we are familiar with existed only a fraction of the time since the first inhabitants arrived 12,000 years ago.

Indians in North America are divided into two categories, prehistoric and historic. Prehistoric signifies the long period before European settlers arrived.

PREHISTORIC INDIANS DIFFERED FROM HISTORIC INDIANS IN THE FOLLOWING WAYS:

They had dogs but no horses, cows, pigs or other domesticated animals.

Archaeological diggings prove there were horses before the prehistoric Indians' arrival, but like the mastodon and tiger they became, for unknown reasons, extinct before the arrival of the Indians.

Horses used by the Indians we have come to know were used only after the arrival of the European explorers.

NO POTTERY

They cooked by the process of stone boiling. This was accomplished by using a deer skin with its edges held up by stakes so that it sagged in the center. It was then filled with water and meat; hot clay balls were placed in the water. After many clay balls were inserted over a long period of time (depending on the amount of meat), the meat was finally cooked.

BURIAL

Burial was not on stilts as depicted in the movies. The prehistoric Indians originally built cone-shaped burial mounds where the bodies were placed sitting upright, with their knees drawn up under their chins (fetal position). It is noteworthy that early Greeks also buried their dead in the fetal position. Burial mounds have been found in various locations throughout the state. In Jonesville, located in Catahoula Parish, there are remains of a great number of temples surrounded by walls and ditches. There are also two large Indian mounds on the

Louisiana State University campus in Baton Rouge. Another unique mound lies on the shore of Grand Lake in Cameron Parish. It is made of clam shells. What makes it unique is not that it is built of clam shells but it is 500 feet long and built in the shape of an alligator. Today the body, tail and three legs of the giant alligator are all that remain.

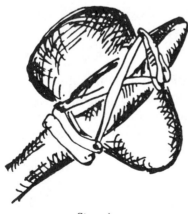

Stone Axe

NO BOWS AND ARROWS

Prehistoric Indians used spears and atlatls to throw them. They also used bolas to bring down game such as buffalo, deer, bear and moose.

Stone axes were used by prehistoric Indians. Metal axes, like the horse, came into use with the coming of the Europeans.

HISTORIC INDIANS

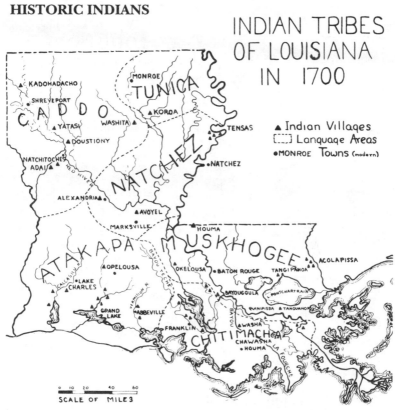

INDIAN TRIBES
OF LOUISIANA
IN 1700

▲ Indian Villages
[....] Language Areas
●MONROE Towns (modern)

SCALE OF MILES

In the 1700s, there were roughly 13,000 Indians living in Louisiana. They made up twenty tribes that spoke six different languages.

Today, there are 1,500 Indians still living in the state. They live in small tribes in six widely separated settlements. Many are not pure Indians, but are mixed with other races.

The largest tribe today is the Houmas. Nearly one thousand members live along the bayous south of Houma, in Terrebonne Parish. The Atakapa Tribe can be found living in the Lake Charles area (Atakapa means cannibal). It is believed that many of the tribes joined forces at one time and almost annihilated the Atakapas for the havoc they were creating amongst all the tribes.

INDIAN GROUPS
OF LOUISIANA
TODAY

JENA • TOWNS (MODERN)
CHOCTAW TRIBES

Near Charenton, in St. Mary Parish, are members of the Chitemachas. South of Marksville in Avoyelles Parish, you will find members of the Tunica Tribe. In Allen Parish, live the Coushattas. The last of the tribes still living in Louisiana are the Choctaws. Some live near the town of Lacombe in St. Tammany Parish, while others live near Jena in LaSalle Parish.

There are yet other Indians who live among white and black citizens and are not living with any of the above mentioned tribes.

Note:

Statistics of today's Indians were compiled from 1980 records.

LOUISIANA INDIANS VISIT PARIS AND THE KING

Shortly after New Orleans was founded, the Duc d' Orleans (the man for whom New Orleans was named), as well as members of his fun loving and frivolous court, expressed an interest in seeing some of the red-skinned Americans that French colonists spoke so much about.

In 1725, an Indian chief and princess, along with twelve warriors, were induced into going to Paris. This was not an easy task, for the ocean was unknown to the Indians. Their fears were quieted both by lies and extravagant promises. They were told the ocean was only a big salt lake. They were also told that France was a land with golden streets, massive flowing fountains, glittering crystal, gorgeous women and men who looked like gods.

In early July, a grand party lasting several days was held for the Indians in New Orleans. The festivities consisted of feasting, drinking, entertainment and smoking of the peace pipe. The latter was to appease the Indians. Before departing, the Indians, to their delight, were given many gifts to help take their minds off the long voyage ahead. The ocean trip took five long months, with the party arriving in Paris in November. From Paris they were taken directly to the Palace at Versailles. On November 16th at the Palace, the creme de la creme of the French court met the Indians for the first time. The Duc d' Orleans was impressed with the chief who stood six feet tall with a perfectly proportioned physique. The Duc also thought him to be most dignified. The princess, on the other hand, was small, delicately formed and very beautiful. The Indian chief, with many hours of practice, gave an elegant and proper salute to the Duc d' Orleans. The Duc acknowledged the salute half heartedly. He wasted no time getting down to business. Through an interpreter, he questioned the chief as to how many men could he put in immediate availability to aid his country against all enemies. The chief, without hesitation, quickly

answered 16,000. The Duc smiled with approval. The chief's face mimicked the Duc's face. Before leaving, the Duc ordered the officers to show their guests anything that might satisfy them and to treat them well. The Indians asked for an audience with the king. The king, a very young boy, was as eager to meet them as they were to meet him. The Indians presented the king with gifts. He in return gave them gifts. After seeing the gardens of the palace and the fountains, the formalities ended and the fun began. The Indians then became the sensation of Paris. The French women of the court, bored perhaps, or merely perverse in their intent, took charge of the chief. Although there was a language barrier, there is a universal

language in smiles, beckoning and inclinations of the head. The Indians had the time of their lives. To the amazement of everyone, the Indians in their normal dress (almost without clothing), put on the first show of its kind at Versailles. The crowd was ecstatic. The king ordered that proper clothes be given them immediately. The Indians for the first time wore knee britches, flowered coats with frills, and cocked hats. The Indian women were laced into corsets, put into fancy French dresses, and wore their hair high and powdered. In place of the regular crude paint, they were given "beauty spots". One night at the opera, the Indians got carried away. At the end of the performance, they stripped themselves of their clothes and

entertained the court with unbelievably fast rhythmic, fascinating gyrations of the Indian dance. Men and women appeared almost in "a state of nature". The French were captivated and did their best to mimic the Indian dances. In appreciation they treated the Indians as if they were royalty. Their every wish, no matter how ridiculous was granted. For a brief time, the Indians were the talk of Paris. The Indian drama reached its climax in the Notre Dame de Paris. In the dimly lit cathedral, with the entire French court in attendance, and all the Indians in fitting French costumes, yet all barefoot, the Indian princess was formally baptized. She threw aside her heathen gods and embraced Christianity. After the baptism, she was married to French Sergeant Dubois. Dubois was immediately elevated to the rank of Captain. At the same time, the princess received the title of Madam. The newlyweds were loaded down with presents of silks, satins and jewels; even the king sent a present.

The planned visit had been more of a success than anyone ever dreamed possible. A huge crowd went to the ship to see the Indians off. They were pleased to see their guests were still in their elegant French clothes, yet still barefoot. The Indians happily sailed back to their native land, Louisiana.

Upon arriving in Louisiana with his new bride, Captain

Dubois was appointed commandant of a fort. One day, not long after their return, Madam Dubois helped her tribe make a surprise attack on the fort. The entire garrison was massacred, including Captain Dubois, the princess's husband. After being killed, he was just like all the others, scalped. Madam Dubois then stripped herself of her corset, elegant French dress, beauty spot, as well as her Christian religion and title of Madam. With one loud yell, she tossed aside her crucifix and again embraced her heathen gods. Naked, happy, and still barefoot, she returned to the wilderness, a princess again.

The Grand Expedition's Route that Ended for DeSoto
on the banks of the Mississippi, Opposite
Present-day Natchez.

DISCOVERY OF LOUISIANA

Louisiana, in spite of being inhabited by man for over 50,000 years, was not officially discovered until 1682. The early explorers from Asia did not even consider or know of a need to make such a claim. When the European explorers arrived (such as Hernando De Soto, the man who is credited in 1541 with discovering what is now called the Mississippi River), they were looking for gold, silver and precious gems. They had plenty of land; hence, they passed through the area and, not finding what they were looking for, pressed on. Little did they realize that far below the ground was a product that would ultimately be more precious in value than any of the above-mentioned exotic metals or stones. Oil today, because of its value, is called "Black Gold" by those in the industry. Never before in recorded history has there ever been a product that has made as many billionaires as oil.

The interesting story as to how, when and why Louisiana was discovered is as follows: In the 15th century, a most capable young French Canadian named Rene Robert Cavelier, Sieur de LaSalle was in a sense looking for action. As a highly successful military leader, he acquired substantial wealth in the service of his king. While there was a lull in the need for his military genius, he searched for adventure, for idleness was not one of LaSalle's pleasures. He preferred action. The greater the challenge and variety the better.

Having great respect for the Indians' knowledge of the land, he was in awe of stories told by them of a great river called by the Indians "Malbenchi," meaning "the great one." He was advised that the great body of water flowed to the west. No doubt thinking to himself, "Since much of the wealth of the world comes from the Orient, why not get on this great waterway and follow it to its entry into the Pacific Ocean? Once there, I can establish a port city and thereby control the flow of wealth from China to the North American continent." Great thought was put into the feasibility of such an undertaking. If tackled, it would be the biggest gamble of his life. Why would it be a gamble? The answer is simple. Most royalty were so

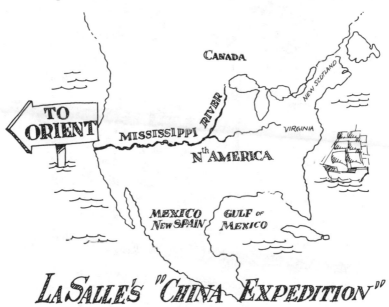

LA SALLE'S "CHINA EXPEDITION"

stingy they squeaked when they walked. When they put their hands out, ninety-nine percent of the time it was to receive, not give. After much soul searching, he decided the project was worth the great financial risk. He sold all of his holdings, used all of his savings, plus borrowed a ton of money to support the eighty people he would need on what he ultimately called the "China Expedition." Since he was headed to the west coast of the North American continent, where he would have an easy jumping-off spot to the Orient, the title he thought was fitting. Beginning in Canada, the explorers made their way through the Great Lakes and ultimately to the great river that was to carry them to their destination. When arriving, LaSalle was favorably impressed by the river. Just as the Indians had described, it was truly a great body of water. As time went by, he began to lose his enthusiasm and finally his confidence in the Indians. He realized that the information furnished by them was erroneous. LaSalle, without question, was a seasoned, bright, highly-capable explorer. In this case, even one far less

capable could have determined they were continually heading south, not west as expected.

Upon arriving at a sharp bend in the river not far from the Gulf of Mexico, LaSalle decided this would be the spot on which the territory would be declared in honor of his illustrious king. On April 9, 1682, a large cross was placed into the fertile soil. This was done because there was no separation of church and state in France. Proper papers were prepared naming this vast territory Louisiane. It consisted of all lands adjacent to all the tributaries that flowed into the mighty river. The territory was so vast that not even 120 years later did men realize its full extent. He named it Louisiane in honor of King Louis XIV. The original spelling by the French, as noted, was with an e at the end. The spelling was later changed by Spain when they took control. Louisiane means "in the realm of Louis." Through the years, the story that has been passed down from generation to generation states that Louisiana was named for Louis the king and Anna the queen. It makes a nice story, but it is historically incorrect. True, Anna was Louis's mother, once the queen of Austria. Unfortunately, she died many years before LaSalle discovered Louisiana. The leader of the expedition was not only a capable man in many fields, he excelled in diplomacy and was well endowed in common sense. He knew that if he received any favors for what he discovered it would come from Louis who was the man carrying the big stick, not Anna who was no longer around to pass out favors.

Once LaSalle verbally proclaimed the land for his king, a rifle salute was fired, papers were signed and notarized, and a toast made to the Sun King. When all the formalities were over, the customary burying of a symbolic item at the base of the cross was at hand. On this occasion, it was a lead plate. The reason: those men who had reached high stations in life proudly showed their achievements by being allowed to eat out of lead plates. LaSalle's plate had the Fleur de Lis — Lily of France (the emblem of France). Unfortunately, today it would be safe to say that almost all school children in Louisiana look at this emblem as the New Orleans Saints football team's emblem, and nothing else.

There has been much controversy over whether LaSalle ever made it to the mouth of the Mississippi River. Some historians say "yea" and others say "nay." I am of the latter belief. One of those who claimed he did make it to the mouth showed proof in the form of a drawing. It showed LaSalle in the bow of a small boat with the mountains of south Louisiana in the background. Need I say more?

Mountains of South Louisiana

LaSalle returned to his home in Canada by the same route he used in making the discovery. From there, he went to France where he had an audience with the king. He was not only awarded, but rewarded for his services. As a reward he was to receive one dollar for every buffalo hide collected on the vast land he had discovered. Had he lived long enough he would have become a very wealthy man. Unfortunately, he did not. On his next journey, his mission was to find the mouth of the Mississippi River. While in the Gulf of Mexico searching for the river's mouth, he made the mistake of staying on the large ship that was unable to get close to the shoreline. Because of this, he was unable to see the river due to mud formations, reeds and shrub trees. He unfortunately passed it by and continued to the west. After some time he realized his mistake. When his ship became grounded, he decided to take a party ashore and backtrack by land. This, he felt, would guarantee his locating the river and ultimately the river's mouth. Once on land they were attacked by the Indians, suffered diseases, and seemed to be going in circles. As time passed, the men began to lose all confidence in their leader. A secret meeting was held whereby it was decided that drastic situations required drastic actions. The final decision; the doctor on the expedition was selected to be the executioner. He waited until the right moment and, when it arrived, he shot LaSalle in the back of the head, killing him instantly.

A huge statue of LaSalle was dedicated in the present state of Texas. Its location is approximately where LaSalle was reported to have been assassinated.

It is ironic that as you travel throughout the state you will find only one small, unimpressive wooden statue (in the city of Kenner) dedicated to the man who discovered not only present-day Louisiana but one-third of the continental United States.

Someone jokingly said, undoubtedly a true blooded Louisianian, that it is only fitting that anyone who is headed for Louisiana and winds up in Texas is always the loser.

DISCOVERY OF THE MOUTH OF THE MISSISSIPPI RIVER

In 1698, Comte de Pontchartrain, the French Marine Minister, decided to move the capital of the Louisiana Territory which was then located in present day Mobile, Alabama. His second goal was to locate the mouth of the Mississippi River. The number one man in his services at that time was Pierre LeMoyne, Sieur d'Iberville. Iberville had not only Pontchartrain's respect but, having never lost a land or naval battle to the English, was highly regarded by them as well.

An expedition to accomplish these two goals was formed with Iberville being selected as its leader. The flotilla consisted of two Man of War ships and two coastal vessels. They left Brest,

France, on October 24, 1698, and did not arrive in Mobile until February 1699. From Mobile, the expedition headed west, where a fort named Maurepas was built on the Gulf Coast. This became the second capital of Louisiana. The site today is Ocean Springs, Mississippi. As the ships moved westward, a number of islands along the coast were named. The great number of dolphins around the first island led to the name Dolphin Island. Later, as a lookout in the crow's nest spotted another island, he blew his horn to notify the captain. He was, no doubt, overly excited, for he blew the horn so hard it came out of his hand and fell into the water. In passing another island, they noticed the skeletal remains of a number of ships

that had been beached by storms. The name Ship Island was recorded in the journal. Passing close to another island, a large number of raccoons were seen roaming the beach. Thinking they were cats, Cat Island became the name inscribed in the

ship's book. As the ships lay at anchor one moonlit night, the moon shined brightly on a series of small islands. Their shimmering in the moonlight made them look like a giant candle-lit chandelier; hence, the name Chandeleur Islands.

On March 3rd, while following the shoreline in six small boats looking for the mouth of the river, a violent storm came up with very little warning. The rough waters became perilous for all in the frail boats. Iberville gave the command for all boats to head into the rock formations on the shoreline. If they stayed out in the rough water, he feared many lives would be lost. As the small boats hit the shoreline expecting to be destroyed by the rocks, they were pleasantly surprised to learn they were not rocks but huge pillows of mud. Iberville cupped his hands, tasted the water, and then he smiled. It was fresh water. By an act of God, he had found the mouth of the Mississippi River. (The huge mud formations were undoubtedly the major reason LaSalle passed up the mouth of the river.) The next day, March 4th, was Shrove Tuesday or Mardi Gras. The flotilla, each boat following behind the other, looked like a small parade as they headed upriver. That night when they made camp at the first great bend in the river, on the eastern side, Iberville recorded the spot as "Mardi Gras Point," the first

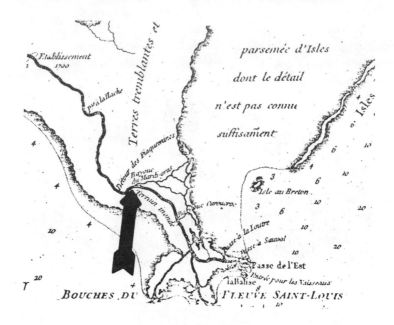

place named on the mainland of Louisiana. Having the presence of mind to name the spot Mardi Gras Point, no doubt they also celebrated Mardi Gras for the first time in Louisiana. Two days later, after battling high winds and a strong current, or slowed down by hangovers from the Mardi Gras celebration, the explorers stopped at a site located on a huge curve of the river. This location, Iberville was told by the Indian guide, was the location of a portage between the river and a large lake that led to the Gulf of Mexico where their ships were anchored. This location was called by the Indians "Chinchuba," meaning alligator. (That is certainly why Chinchuba was selected as the name of the Louisiana Institute For The Deaf, for alligators have no ears.) Buffalo was recorded in the journal as the evening meal. Young Bienville, Iberville's brother, surely must have been impressed with the site, for this is where, two decades later, he located the city of New Orleans. No doubt the Indians shook their heads in disbelief when they realized a town was being built. They believed the location was suitable for alligators, snakes and mosquitos, and nothing else. The next day the party moved directly across the river to the west bank where they were greeted by the Indians at their village. The Indians and their guests ate, smoked the peace pipe and drank the Indians' beer. The Indians raised persimmon trees with the fermented fruit serving to make their fire water. The French word for persimmon is "plaquemines," hence the

name Plaquemines Parish many years later. As the flotilla headed north, it passed an area that was marked with tall, red, wooden poles. This was the Indians' method of marking off their territory. This area today is known as Baton Rouge, French for "red stick." No doubt, the Indians' favorite color was red. Istrouma and Houma both mean red. The Houma Indians went one step further. On their war shields they painted a red crayfish with claws extended as though ready to fight to the death. Farther north, as they were about to enter a great bend in the river, where the current was unbelievably swift, the Indian guide suggested they do as the Indians had always done, that is, pick up their canoes and carry them over land, bypassing the obstacle, and then put their canoes back into the river. This, they later found, saved many, many hours. The French designation for "cut point" is Pointe Coupee (the name of the parish where this occurred). When the decision was made to return to the gulf, the Indians again offered a time-saving suggestion. They recommended using the back entrance to the gulf, thereby saving not hours but days. Iberville instructed his little brother Bienville to return the way they came to double check the Indians' accuracy. It was on the return trip (see page 132) that Detour a l'Anglais — English Turn was entered on the map of Louisiana. Iberville, as suggested by his guide, returned to his ship by way of the back entrance. This is where Bayou Manchac, meaning back entrance, got its name. Upon arriving at a beautiful lake,

Iberville decided to name it Pontchartrain, in honor of the French Marine Minister, the man who sent him on the expedition. Later, upon entering a larger and more beautiful lake, he reevaluated and named the bigger lake Pontchartrain and the smaller one Maurepas for one of Pontchartrain's sons who held the title, Duc d'Maurepas.

Iberville, upon returning to his ships in the Gulf of Mexico, was pleased to know that the Indians were most accurate, for it took Bienville several days longer to arrive back at the ships.

CHAPTER 2

POTPOURRI

INTRODUCTION

This chapter, as the name implies, will cover a multitude of subject matter covering all geographic areas of the state. From the smallest church in the United States to a castle built on a bet. From the largest lumber mill in the world, that brought with it prosperity, to an orchid-like nautical plant that caused economic disaster, and after one hundred years is still a menace. Also covered is the largest lottery in the world in its day, to a ship captain who brought Louisiana an economic pay day. The nation's first air mail service and America's oldest hunting and fishing club. The state's first toll bridge, a religious procession, and would you believe it, the story of a fish in a bag that is now known and enjoyed worldwide. Yes, this chapter even has a story about a ship in a cradle, and when it flies in the sky as well as where and why.

BOGALUSA, LOUISIANA
Largest Sawmill In The World

Charles and Frank Goodyear of Pennsylvania were born to parents of modest means. Through hard work and shrewd business dealings, they became successful in the lumber business in New York.

1,000,000
Board feet per day

In the early 1900s, they could see the end of the lumber supply in New York. At first they considered retiring with their vast fortunes. Six percent interest on their money wasn't good enough, plus both had sons in college and wanted to have something for them to do when they graduated.

Extensive research showed that there was vast timberland in the deep south, a virgin forest yet untapped. Again their first thought was to buy the timberland and hold it for future sale. Again their thoughts were with their sons. After careful study they decided to go ahead with a complete project rather than buying just the land. And what an undertaking it turned out to be! Their project called for construction of the largest sawmill in the world. Research also showed that there would be sufficient lumber involved to justify construction of their own railroad. It was called "The New Orleans Great Northern." An estimate was made of production. A whopping one million board feet per day was projected.

The two brothers were the principal shareholders in the venture. Additional stock was held by Hamlins and Crarys, Pennsylvania capitalists and Charles I. James, heir of an aristocratic Maryland family fortune.

The project was set in motion when the Goodyears sent $1,250,000 on March 8, 1905, to S.D. Lacey and Company of New Orleans with orders to start looking for land.

Later that year, the Goodyears arrived at the plush St. Charles Hotel in New Orleans. This project was so large it required the personal scrutiny of the major investors.

With them was Will Sullivan, the manager of the proposed facility; Jim Lacey, agent hired to buy the land; J.F. Colenman, civil engineer; and Tom Pigott and Jim Whalen, timber estimators and surveyors.

The party crossed Lake Pontchartrain by ferryboat and combed the entire area, including land in Mississippi. A location in Mississippi was originally selected but then rejected because of unfavorable tax laws in that state. In early September the group camped for the night on Bogue Lusa Creek.

"This is my idea of paradise," said Will Sullivan. "There is enough timber here to keep a sawmill operating day and night for 25 years."

The site was further discussed and it was decided that this would become the location of the mill and the new proposed town that they would call Bogalusa, after the Indian words Bogue Lusa, meaning Black Water.

Whalen and Pigott stayed behind after the rest of the party left and started surveying the new site.

Bogalusa was the first sawmill town ever planned and laid out so it would not dry up and blow away when the timber ran out. It was even to have a golf course called Magic City South.

Within five months, construction began on both the new city and the mill. The first building to go up on the Bogue Lusa Creek was affectionately called Blarney's Castle in honor of the Irish superintendent, Will Sullivan.

By the end of 1906, work was ahead of schedule. The population in Bogalusa had grown to 8,000 in a short time, making it the fifth largest city in the entire state. 1906 ushered in the first passenger train, the first circus, the first Model T. Ford and many other firsts for the area. Magic was in the air. Bogalusa and the Great Southern Lumber Company were on their way.

Construction was nearing completion and everyone was ecstatic. The Corliss high pressure steam engine, the heart of the mill, was completely installed. All that needed to be done was the fitting of the leather belt that would drive it. The hides of 720 steers were used to fabricate the largest leather drive belt ever manufactured.

Word went out that November 15, 1907, would be the start up date, but hold on, the panic of 1907 had just begun and a telegram was sent: "Do not start up mill until notified."

The 1907 panic was followed by a business depression, causing further delay.

In the fall of 1908, Superintendent Sullivan was called to a board meeting in New York and asked, "How soon can you start the mill?" He enthusiastically, and without hesitation answered, "Two weeks."

Sullivan got a little carried away for it was six weeks later when the steam fired Corliss engine was given life and the first log put into the carriage and cut with precision. Ben Sellers was recorded as having sawed the first log of the new mill.

Many dignitaries were present but the Goodyear brothers who conceived and financed the largest sawmill in the world, were conspicuous by their absence. Frank had died before the project was completed and Charles, president of the Great Southern Lumber Company, was not well enough to travel.

The Great Southern Lumber Company was successful in

producing the predicted one million board feet per day. Its marketplace, the world. One hundred railroad cars a day of lumber were being shipped throughout the United States. The lumber was also shipped to every continent of the world by way of the Port of New Orleans.

Will Sullivan was right in all of his predictions with the exception of one. The forest was more plentiful than even he thought. He estimated enough lumber was available for 25 years, he missed it by 5 years. Ben Sellers, the man that sawed the first log in the fall of 1908 was recorded again as cutting the last log in April of 1938.

The Goodyear brothers, whose original goal was to give their sons jobs after college, realized their dreams. Both of their sons joined the company, eventually running it. Will Sullivan, the manager, realized his dream too; he became the first mayor of Bogalusa and when the lumber finally ran out, Bogalusa remained a thriving community called, The Magic City of the South.

LOTTERY IN LOUISIANA OLD HAT

"The people of Louisiana have a compulsion for gambling unequaled anywhere in the world that my travels have taken me," wrote C.C. Robin, a nationally acclaimed 19th century writer. "Their compulsion for gambling is only equaled by their compulsion for alcoholic beverages."

It appeared that all indulged in it and, he surmised, that possibly the prevalence of the habit arose from lack of education and stimulating intellectual activity.

In the history of Louisiana, virtually every form of gambling has been utilized at one time or another. Two of the most popular games of chance today, poker and craps, had their beginnings in Louisiana. Betting on horse racing, cock fights, jai-alai, keno and bingo, along with every other form of gambling, legal or illegal, were and still are, a part of our everyday lives.

Today there is again strong talk of having a legal lottery operated by the state to generate funds.

Lottery is far from being a new source of government revenue. In 1614, long before there was a United States of America, the English colonies on the East Coast were financed by a lottery operated by the Virginia Co., the managing firm of the colonies. The winner, in 1614, received a hefty 4,500 crowns, a tidy sum in its day.

The United States of America won their Independence on July 4, 1776. Nine months later the U.S. Congress held its first

lottery in Philadelphia. Proceeds from the lottery were used to help finance the newly formed government.

In Louisiana it is not known when the first lottery was held, but records show that, as early as 1820, a lottery was used by the Presbyterian Church to pay off a $45,000 debt.

Whenever you speak of lottery in Louisiana, you cannot leave out the Louisiana State Lottery Company. It was the number one lottery in the world in its day in generating profit. Its success has never been equaled.

In 1868, shortly after the Civil War ended, the carpetbag government was in control. Charles T. Howard of New Orleans and his New York capitalist friend, John A. Morris, were successful in getting a 25 year monopoly to operate a lottery from the administration of Republican Governor Henry Clay Warmoth. For this exclusive franchise, Louisiana was to receive $40,000 a year to help operate Charity Hospital.

For several years, profits were slim to nonexistent. Lottery competition from other states was fierce. Howard and Morris were seriously considering throwing in the towel. But along came Dr. Maxmilian A. Dauphin, an Irish political exile.

Dauphin took a small job with the Louisiana State Lottery. With his experiences with successful lotteries, Dauphin made a proposal to the owners that he guaranteed would bring them enormous wealth. Dauphin's very persuasive manner made Howard and Morris realize the shrewdness of the plan. They took the gamble an it paid off handsomely.

Dauphin realized that dramatic publicity guaranteeing the honesty of the operation was the secret. In 1877, he drew two well-known heroes of the Confederacy, General P.G.T. Beauregard of Louisiana and General Jubal A. Early of Virginia into the scheme. For their services as commissioners and supervisors of drawings, they each received $30,000 a year. The drawings, were open to the public, and were well advertised and conducted with unimpeachable fairness.

When Dauphin took over the operation, tickets were 25 cents and the top prize was $3,750. In short order, business increased at a rapid, even runaway speed. Ticket prices rose to $40 each — you could buy a portion of a ticket — and the prize of $600,000 was tax free. The lottery began to operate nationally and internationally. There were daily, weekly and finally, the big monthly drawings.

By 1890, 45 percent of all New Orleans postal receipts were

lottery-related. Lottery business coming through the mail hit $25 million a year, tax free. All the operating expenses of the lottery were paid with the take from the daily lottery.

Finally, Congress passed a law prohibiting the use of the mail for the transmission of lottery related business. It was to be the lottery's death blow.

Leading citizens, especially political enemies and religious leaders, formed an anti-lottery campaign to rid the state of the "debaucher of politics and debaser of the people." The nickname given the Louisiana State Lottery Co. was "the octopus," whose tentacles went deep into the pockets of the

THE LOTTERY OCTOPUS

poor and entwined the necks of the legislators who could be bought.

The campaign was persistent and by 1892, the Louisiana State Lottery had drawn its final number. What was to be a 25-year monopoly ended one year short of full term.

In its 24 years, not one person ever won the $600,000 prize. A New Orleans barber did win $300,000 for a half ticket.

HOUMA BLIMP BASE

At the beginning of World War II, ships in the Gulf of Mexico, without any protection, were sitting ducks for German U-Boats. U-Boats became so brazen, they sat at the mouth of the River and sank ships as they entered the Gulf waters.

The United States decided to build a $14,000,000 blimp base in Houma, Louisiana that would accommodate six 254 foot long airships, complete with radar, communication, machine guns for protection and depth charges for attack. These giants of the skies would organize ships to move in convoys and give aerial surveillance.

The monstrous all wooden hangar (steel not available) to house the blimps was built by W. Horace Williams Co. of New Orleans. The building was 1000 feet long, 300 feet wide and 212 feet high. The 50 ton doors were unique in that they were the only detached domed-shaped doors ever built on any blimp hangar. It took 17 diesel trucks to open them and store them alongside the hangar.

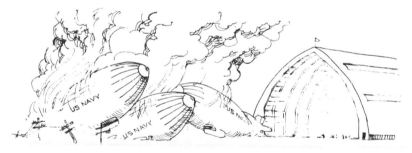

APRIL 21, 1944

When commissioned on May 1, 1943, Blimp Squadron 22 had 30 officers, 100 enlisted men, and 35 marines.

Two tragedies struck the base in a three day period in 1944. On April 19, Airship K-133, while on duty over the Gulf with a 10 man crew, was hit by a violent, unexpected wind storm. After a 40 minute struggle against the elements K-133 crashed into the Gulf. Only Ensign William Thewes survived. He was taken from the rough waters 21 hours later, 20 miles from where the ship went down. Two days later, April 21, at 4:15 a.m., unexpected 60 mph winds hit the base and tore through the hangar causing a venturi effect. Three blimps parted their mooring lines and deck pendents and were blown out of the hangar. One hit high tension wires and struck the ground. All three caught fire immediately. Eye witnesses said the sight was like "Dante's Inferno." The three ships, each filled with 1/2 billion cubic feet of gas, burned with the same brilliance as the sun itself. It was a scene one would never forget.

Blimp Squadron 22 was decommissioned September 21, 1944. In 1947, because of high maintenance costs, 1/2 ton of dynamite was strategically placed throughout the hangar and detonated. The huge building was leveled to the ground in only six seconds.

FIRST AIR MAIL SERVICE — ALMOST

April 12, 1912, was a red-letter day for all Louisianians. Airmail service between New Orleans and Baton Rouge was to become a reality. Aviator George Mestach, after being sworn in as a mail carrier, hopped into the open cockpit of his Borel-Mathis airplane. After a lengthy delay because of inclement weather, he took off, with 32 pounds of the nation's first air mail. As he took off he smiled and waved to the crowd. They didn't take their eyes off the aircraft for a long time. The reason, George was having a problem gaining altitude. He had to circle the field a number of times to gain the necessary altitude before he was able to start on his journey. The crowd didn't seem to mind. They strained their eyes to read the sign on the wings of his aircraft, U. S. Mail. The next problem to surface occurred when the wind pressure broke one of the glasses on George's goggles. No big problem; he made the rest of the trip using one eye. This unfortunately created another problem. Around Lutcher, George lost his way and had to circle the area until he got his bearings. Once he was oriented, he continued on his history-making journey. At 5:41 p.m., one hour and 31 minutes after leaving New Orleans, he had

reached his destination. George was over the LSU athletic field looking down at the cheering and waving crowd. He cut off the engine and circled the field. The crowd gasped as he came in for the landing. Would he clear the fence? Oh no! His plane plowed into the fence knocking it over. One of the fence posts did serious damage to the plane, as well as inflicting cuts on George's body from his face to his lower legs. When they finally got to him, George was still holding the mail bag with a tight grip. Still groggy, he was helped from the aircraft and gave the pouch to the Baton Rouge Postmaster. Mission accomplished, in spite of a few minor mishaps.

Although the return trip was cancelled because of obvious reasons, the nation's first airmail was delivered as scheduled on April 12, 1912.

Without trying to sound like "Can you top this?" Washington D.C.'s first airmail delivery was a doozy. On May 15, 1918, the U. S. Post Office Department was to inaugurate what was billed as "The world's first airmail service" (even though airmail had already been delivered successfully as pointed out). It was to be a big step for the U. S. Post Office Department — big enough that President Woodrow Wilson and other high-ranking government officials were at the large polo field in Potomac Park to witness the event. At precisely 11:00 a.m., the scheduled time, pilot George Boyle entered the cockpit. Unfortunately, the engine would not start. Mechanics worked frantically. As time passed, the President became impatient and highly

irritated. Someone checked the fuel tanks and found that they were empty. The tanks were filled, and Boyle finally took off. But, instead of flying north to Philadelphia, his first scheduled stop, he followed the wrong set of railroad tracks and flew southeasterly. Intending to ask directions he touched down near Waldorf, Maryland, 20 miles from Washington, D.C. The landing was rough, damaging the propeller. Unable to get off the ground again, his 140 pounds of airmail had to be delivered by truck to Philadelphia and by plane to New York.

FIRST AIRMAIL STAMP

Just as the inaugural airmail flights in Louisiana and Washington, D.C., seemed jinxed, the first airmail stamp was also snake bitten. The stamp had an engraving of a Curtiss "Jenny" that had been printed upside down.

HARVEY CASTLE

Ship captain Joseph Hale Harvey, a Virginian, in the course of his work frequented the port of New Orleans. In 1845, he fell in love with and married Louise, the oldest daughter of prosperous Nicholas Noel Destrehan. Destrehan gave his daughter and future son-in-law a wedding gift consisting of land and a canal across the river from New Orleans (present day Harvey). Destrehan had the canal constructed in 1835 almost entirely by slaves who used spades as their only tools.

This barren piece of land and little-used canal, through the efforts of Joseph Hale Harvey, in later years were to be transformed into a beehive of activity with a building that would become a landmark.

Harvey was a colorful character. Like most river men, he was a great talker. In 1844, shortly before he and Louise were married, they were having dinner at the Destrehan Plantation with some of Nicholas Noel Destrehan's friends. As was the custom, after dinner the ladies retired to one parlor to have coffee, do needlepoint and entertain themselves in conversation. The men adjoined to a separate parlor where they smoked cigars, drank brandy and played cards. During

"MY DEEP LOVE FOR YOU MAKES IT POSSIBLE FOR ME TO ACCOMPLISH WHAT ALL THOUGHT IMPOSSIBLE."

the conversation, Harvey, no doubt very much in love with Louise, openly expressed his feelings about his bride to be. He stated that he loved her to the point he could accomplish what some had said would be impossible. One of the Creole gentlemen present expressed need for further explanation. Harvey responded without hesitation. He could, as an example, build a castle for the woman he loved in only ninety days. "You are right, my friend," said the Creole gentleman. "This is something that cannot be accomplished. You have let your heart overtake common sense and that which is reality."

Harvey could not let this man question his undying love and what he could accomplish in expressing his love for Louise. Before the evening was over, a substantial wager was made between the two gentlemen.

Harvey wasted no time. He assembled a construction force of free Negroes who lived in a community called Free Town located close to the canal where the structure was to be built. A contractor, with Louise's assistance, was consulted as to the design of the building. In short order, all was ready and work began. The three-story structure, with eighteen foot ceilings, had ten large rooms on each floor, plus spacious hallways. The first two floors had wide galleries that ran entirely around the house. From the center of the great hall, which extended to the rear of the building, rose a grand twin staircase with beautiful walnut balustrade. The double stairways were unique, for they united at a landing midway between the first and second floors. This was, of course, symbolic of the joining in marriage of Captain Harvey and Louise. To save some time, while the building was being constructed, furnishings were simultaneously being assembled. They consisted of marble mantles, elaborate friezes, velvet hangings and imported pictures making the interior indeed castle like. The massive structure was topped with two towering octagon-shaped ornamental turrets on each side. The towers afforded an unobstructed view of the river and for years served as a landmark for river pilots. Finishing touches to the project were the construction of extensive gardens with circular winding walks and glass-enclosed conservatories. All that has been described above was completed within the time constraints of the bet of ninety days.

Louise was ecstatic. Her husband-to-be, because of his deep love for her, had accomplished what most felt was the impossible. Harvey was, no doubt, equally pleased, for now he had a home for his bride, built to fulfill her every desire. He also won a great deal of money and proved that true love can conquer all.

As someone later stated, maybe he just dreaded the thought of having to live with his in-laws. The Harveys lived in the beautiful as well as functional castle until 1870. After that, it served as a courthouse for Jefferson Parish and an entertainment center using the name Columbia Gardens. In its later years, it became a tenement house.

In 1924, the Harvey family sold the canal and castle with all lands to the U.S. Government for $425,000.00. In May of 1929, the U.S. Government tore down the castle and began work on the Harvey locks, completing them in 1933.

"THE QUEEN"
LOUISE DESTREHAN HARVEY

Louise Destrehan Harvey was affectionately referred to by her friends as "The Queen". Born into an enormously wealthy creole family and married to flamboyant Joseph Hale Harvey, Louise had not only the aristocratic background but the financial backing to play the part with little effort. Louise was proud of and loved the home (castle) her husband built to show his undying love for her. Large dinners and exquisite parties were enjoyed on a regular basis at the castle. Louise, being the socialite that she was, was also invited to numerous social gatherings during the year at plantations located on the rivers and bayous of south Louisiana. For her own convenience, as well as the convenience of her invited guests, she built a dock on the Mississippi River adjacent to her castle. It was long enough to dock not one but two elaborate barges she designed and had built. To overcome the swift current of the mighty Mississippi River, each barge was propelled by oars operated by fifty powerful slaves. When wind conditions were favorable, propulsion was supplemented by sail power. The barges were specifically designed for the convenience of Louise and her guests. Each was large enough to carry several carriages, as well as the horses needed to pull them. Yes, the Nile may have had its Queen Cleopatra and her famous barge, but the Mississippi River had "The Queen", Louise Destrehan Harvey, who had not one but two royal barges at her disposal.

LOUISIANA'S FIRST TOLL BRIDGE

The City of New Orleans covers 365 square miles. Of this, 166 square miles are covered by water in the form of rivers, bayous, streams, swamps and marshes. With this startling statistic, it is why, even though we have had more than our share of rain, mosquitoes, roaches and, in recent years, losing seasons by the New Orleans Saints, for a long time we had a scarcity of bridges.

Bridges were necessary in New Orleans almost from the very beginning. The first bridges were wooden foot bridges located in the French Quarter. When a city is below sea level with 58.16" of rain per year, with no mechanical means of getting rid of the water in the early years, it is easy to understand why foot bridges were necessary.

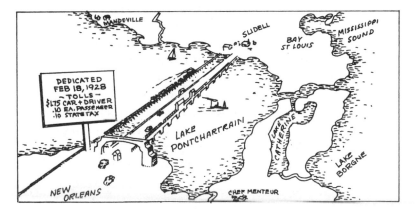

For the first 210 years of its existence, New Orleans was a peninsula. To get into the city from the north, south, and east, you had to use ferry boats.

In 1928, the watery obstacle to the east of the city was about to be eliminated. In the early 1920s, automobiles and trucks became even more popular. In 1927 alone, the United States manufactured 3 1/2 million vehicles. Throughout the United States, crossing waterways became not only time consuming and a nuisance, but crippling to commerce. Studies by a private eastern company proved there was profit to be made by constructing a toll bridge to the east of New Orleans across Lake Pontchartrain.

The first toll bridge in North America was built in 1654 in a town today called Rowley, Massachusetts. This bridge was unique as a toll bridge as there was no charge for people to cross, but a toll was charged for each animal crossing the bridge. The company that was to build Louisiana's first toll bridge was called the Louisiana Pontchartrain Bridge Company with Ely P. Watson as president. One of the prime contractors selected was the McWilliams Company. This was to be no small undertaking. The 5 1/2-million-dollar bridge, and roadways connecting Orleans and St. Tammany Parishes, when completed, would be the longest concrete bridge in the world. Because it was the first of its kind to be constructed, using 3,000 pre-stressed concrete piles 2 feet square, 74 feet long, (driven by Raymond Concrete Pile Company) a special pile driver had to be designed and built to construct the 4.78 miles, 35 foot wide bridge with two draw spans. Construction moved along like precision clockwork. The bridge was completed in just 417 days, many months ahead of the projected completion date.

The official dedication took place on Saturday, February 18, 1928. Louisiana Governor Simpson, Governor-Designate Huey P. Long, New Orleans Mayor Arthur J. O'Keefe, mayors of most of the cities in St. Tammany Parish, and mayors of many cities along the gulf coast all the way to Florida were present. Speakers emphasized the opening was a monument to the new aggressive spirit that had taken hold of New Orleans. One speaker said it proved, in a material way, the faith of investors and the soundness of the city's future. Travel time to and from New Orleans over the new span would be reduced considerably, and would enhance trade between New Orleans and the manufacturing cities in the Northeast, cited another speaker. It was also projected that the population of Slidell would triple in less than ten years. After all scheduled speakers said what they had to say, the ribbon was cut, and vehicles sped across the span for the first time. The toll on Louisiana's first toll bridge was the same as it cost to cross the waterway by ferry, $1.25 per vehicle and driver, plus 10 cents for each additional passenger. There was one additional charge added to cross the bridge, and that was a 10 cent state tax per vehicle.

Over the years, the bridge has had a number of different names. Originally, it was called the Pontchartrain Bridge. It was also referred to as the great Watson-Williams Pontchartrain Bridge — Watson was president of the company that built it, and Williams one of the major contractors. Since it was close to five miles long, 4.78 miles, it was called by some the Five Mile Bridge.

When Huey Long became the governor of Louisiana, knowing the importance of smooth movement of traffic, especially commerce, he built 431 bridges during his administration. He was vehemently opposed to toll bridges and offered to have the state buy the Highway 11, Lake Pontchartrain Bridge. He was emphatically told "NO" by the owners of the bridge. Huey, in his own inimitable way, found the solution to the obstacle. On Highway 90, just a short distance from the toll bridge, a free state bridge was constructed over the Rigolets. In 1938, not being able to compete with the free Highway 90 crossing, Highway 11 Lake Pontchartrain Toll Bridge became a free state-owned bridge. (Louisiana purchased the 5.5 million dollar bridge and access roadways for $940,000.) At this time, it took on yet another name, the Maestri Bridge, after Bob Maestri, the then Mayor of New Orleans, and a staunch supporter of Huey Long.

Of the 15,150 state bridges in Louisiana — this does not include parish bridges — only three have tolls on them, namely, The Greater New Orleans twin span, the Sunshine Bridge, and Lake Pontchartrain Causeway.

After 61 years, the Highway 11 Lake Pontchartrain Bridge, or whatever name you choose to call it, is still the seventh longest bridge in Louisiana.

WORLD'S SMALLEST CHURCH
BAYOU GOULA, LOUISIANA

St. Peter's Basilica in Rome, with a seating capacity of over 6,000 is generally accepted as the largest church in the world. On the other end of the spectrum, the smallest is the Madonna Church of Bayou Goula, Louisiana with a seating capacity of zero.

This small church was the outcome of an incident that took place in 1890. A poor cane farmer named Anthony Goullo prayed to the Blessed Mother to intercede on behalf of his son who was seriously ill. The son did recover and in appreciation Mr. Goullo immediately placed an order in Italy for a statue of The Assumption of Our Lady, which upon arrival he proudly displayed in his home. Over the years, many friends who visited his home suggested and encouraged him to build a chapel to house the beautiful statue of the Blessed Mother. In 1905, Mr. Goullo donated a piece of land for a church; people of the community donated the materials, and his neighbor Saveria Cascio did the actual work. The original building was a 7 foot octagonal shape cypress building. Upon completion, Mr. Goullo was very proud of the church with its small altar, tiny stained glass window, small rooftop cross, and the glass encased statue of Mary, the Mother of Jesus.

The church was officially dedicated in 1905 with a solemn mass. Of course the date was August 15, the feast day of the Assumption of the Blessed Mother. Every year since, on August 15, mass is celebrated in the tiny structure that is only large enough to accommodate the priest and two altar boys. A tall man could stretch his arms and touch any wall of the chapel while standing in the center of the church.

Although there were just a handful of people (all on the outside of the church building) at the first mass, over the years the crowds have grown to hundreds and hundreds, all still standing, or sitting on benches outside the church. Many bring their umbrellas to protect themselves from the relentless heat of the sun. The large crowd that continues to grow only proves that the church may be tiny, but its popularity is as big as life.

In 1916, the Goullo family moved to Illinois but other local families took over care of the church. In 1925, a new levee had to be built requiring the church to be relocated. When this was done, Joseph Polozola changed the design to its present rectangular shape and enlarged it to eight feet long by six feet wide. Even with the enlargement it still holds the record of the world's smallest church and, yes, its seating capacity is still zero.

The people of Bayou Goula are proud of the church and are quick to point out it is not just a roadside chapel. A vigil light burns in the church every day of the year; it has the annual August 15 mass, the rosary is recited every day in May, the month of Mary, and again from August 1st through 15th.

Although the only door of the little church is locked when not in use, the key is plainly visible in a box that hangs on the side of the structure.

Records indicate that almost every day of the year either local people or visitors from the United States and various parts of the world stop at the smallest church in the world to pray, meditate and, before leaving, sign the register. Possibly they find that the smallness of the church allows them to be closer to the altar of God and offers a solace as abiding as that of St. Peter's Cathedral, the largest church in the world.

The Madonna Church of Bayou Goula reinforces the old saying — good things come in little packages.

WATER HYACINTHS — BEAUTY AND THE BEAST

At the 1884 New Orleans World's Fair, the largest horticultural structure ever built for a world's fair housed magnificent gardens from each continent. The Japanese, quick to latch on to a local custom, especially when it served their purpose, enticed fair visitors to their exhibit by offering them lagniappe. Each family who visited their gardens received a package of seeds of the beautiful orchid-like plant of the water hyacinth that was on display. Those who received them were told to place them in ponds and waterways and just forget them. In time they would grow, multiply and bloom, not only in numbers, but in beauty as well.

Grow, multiply and bloom they did. It was soon learned the plant was able to reproduce in ways and on a scale that are frightening in their ramifications. It was learned that a single plant could produce 65,000 others in a single season. One acre of flowering hyacinths could produce anywhere from fifty to eight hundred million seeds. The plants, with the aid of birds and storms, spread like wildfire. More disastrous information was learned when research showed 900,000 hyacinth plants could float in just one acre of water. Beautiful as they are above

the water with their magnificent orchid-like purple flower, it is just the opposite under the water line. Below the surface, the vegetation is dependent on light! Photosynthesis, the process by which plants use energy from the sun to produce food, is not possible. The plants below the hyacinths die. Phytoplankton disappears and with it the fish. The pond weeds upon which ducks feed go and, so, of course, do the ducks. The final blow came when many of the navigable waterways in Louisiana, because of the hyacinths were no longer navigable.

By 1897, things had gone from bad to worse. All local attempts to rid the waterways of this menace were futile. The U. S. Corps of Engineers with all their expertise was summoned. Their attempts would have made an excellent T.V. comedy had T.V. been around then.

The Corps quickly sized up the situation and couldn't understand what all the fuss was about. The solution, as they saw it, was simple. Hundreds of men with pitchforks would scoop the hyacinths out of the water and throw them on the banks to rot and die. The problem with this approach was that while they were being thrown out to rot and die, others were reproducing faster than ever as the water was cleared.

In 1900, a sternwheeler was brought, at some expense and difficulty, into the bayous. It had a four-foot conveyor belt attachment that picked up the hyacinths, chewed them into pulp and spit them out. The result was disappointing, and history showed that the men who were trying to get rid of the flower understandably lost their tempers; they soon turned to dynamite. The wilderness boomed with explosion after explosion. Everything in the immediate vicinity of each explosion was destroyed — everything but the hyacinths, thanks to the redoubtable ability of their seeds to sprout after long dormancy. A bayou can be completely clear on the surface and can stay clear for a number of years; then the seeds germinate and the hyacinths rise again — and very soon after that the bayou is once more covered by a mass of flowers.

After dynamite proved useless, a flame thrower was paddled

into the bayous. Louisiana Conservationist, published by the Louisiana Wildlife and Fisheries Commission, carried an account: "A full cone of fire, hot enough to melt a block of steel, was squirted on a hyacinth raft. When the fuel was exhausted, a frog emerged from the blackened mat and began sunning itself. The scientist using the flame thrower was even more astounded later during the next growing season. The burnt plants were not only the first to sprout, but also averaged nine inches taller than surrounding plants."

The next attempt was in the form of arsenic. Some of this got into the food of the workers at the site and resulted in the death of one man and critical illness to thirteen others. The hyacinths grew on.

Today the water hyacinth is kept under control, to a certain extent, with vigilance and the expenditure of substantial sums of money. But they remain fixed inhabitants of the bayou country. And yes, they are still as beautiful as they are troublesome.

POMPANO en PAPILLOTE
AND OTHER TASTY HISTORICAL DISHES

Louisiana's love of good food has been the catalyst for a number of local dishes. Examples are as follows: the popular King Cake is symbolic of Mardi Gras and carnival. With 500,000 plus being sold each year during the carnival season and Mardi Gras, I think it is safe to say this is an accepted tradition.

The poorboy sandwich was created during the long, economically devastating transit strike. With little money to be spent, Clovis and Denny Martin did their part to help the poor boys by offering them a sandwich large enough to feed their families for only a nickel. It was appropriately called the "Poorboy." This delicacy has been eaten every day of the week in astronomical numbers ever since its introduction to New Orleans. The Italian equivalent to the popular poorboy was invented at Central Grocery, and named "muffuletta," taking its name from the bread it was made on.

Antoine's, the oldest family-owned restaurant in the world,

was founded in New Orleans in 1840. It is located at 713-717 St. Louis Street in the historic French Quarter. It was here that history was made when the wealthiest man in the world, an American named John D. Rockefeller, was acknowledged by Antoines as being the richest man in the world with a dish concocted in his honor. It was called "Oysters Rockefeller." It was appropriately labeled this, for it was considered the richest flavor in the world for the richest man in the world. This is the number one dish at Antoine's. Over 10 million of these delicacies have been served since its inception.

Another man honored by Antoine's was one of the greatest hot-air balloonists in the world. He was a Frenchman who was

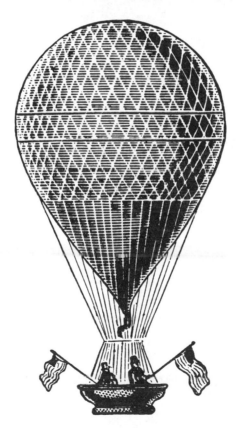

considered one of, if not the greatest balloonist in his day. Stories about his fancy stunts on errant air waves at the French Army maneuvers were printed in newspapers all over the world. Jules Alciatore, proprietor of Antoine's, upon learning that this famous balloonist planned on dining at his world-famous restaurant, went to work to prepare a unique dish suitable for this great guest. His answer to the challenge was the introduction in North America of cooking in a paper bag. The heat generated during cooking caused the bag to inflate, thereby obtaining the look of a hot air balloon. The new dish prepared for the Frenchman was appropriately named "Pompano en Papillote." This style of cooking had yet another plus. By being cooked in a sealed bag the fish retained its seductive flavors.

Although the balloonist dined indoors at Antoine's restaurant, he must have been flying high that evening. He was served a new dish fashioned to resemble his hot air balloon, plus the dish was named in his honor. It has become one of the most asked for dishes at Antoine's.

Just as the air streams carry hot air balloons all over the globe, the uniqueness and exquisite flavor of Pompano en Papillote has also traveled. Today it is served at many of the great restaurants around the world.

KENNER, LOUISIANA — St. Rosalie Procession

This year marks the 85th anniversary of the above solemn and colorful celebration. The answers to when and how it all came about are as follows.

In the 10th century, a girl named Rosalie was born to a wealthy Sicilian family. As a young girl she rejected the luxuries available to her and lived as a hermit in a cave three miles from her home in Palermo. Here she totally dedicated her life to the services of God through prayer, meditation and self denial. Rosalie died in 1160, but the memory of her devotion was passed on from generation to generation. In 1625, Sicily was besieged by the plague. As thousands died, the devout Sicilians prayed to Rosalie to intercede in their behalf to stop their sufferings. Their prayers were answered and the plague ended.

Pope Urban VII ordered St. Rosalie's (the patron saint of the plague) feast day be inserted into the church calendar as September 4.

In 1899, the community of Kenner (mostly Sicilians) who earned their livelihoods as farmers were not themselves besieged by the plague, but their horses and cattle were. They had not forgotten their beloved Rosalie and prayed to her again. They promised to place a statue of her in their parish church, Our Lady of Prompt Succor, and hold a procession in her honor each year if she would intercede for them again. Again, their prayers were answered. To fulfill their promise, a statue was procured immediately and in 1900, a procession was planned for September 9, the Sunday after her feast day.

The festivities started with the 7:00 a.m. mass and a capacity crowd of 500 in the church, including an entire brass band. A few remarks were made in English referencing St. Rosalie's life, followed by a sermon in Italian by Rev. Pasquale Bavasso who expounded on the life of St. Rosalie. He then blessed the banner of the society "Fratelanza Italiana di Santa Rosalie."

At 12 o'clock noon, the celebrants took dinner, picnic style, followed by music with dancing and liquid libation.

At 4 o'clock, the first St. Rosalie's procession that was promised by the grateful Sicilians of Kenner, started from in front of the church. The procession was led by the priest, followed by a number of men who carried the statue of St. Rosalie, the society banner, the American and Italian flags, and almost the entire community. Most walked barefoot with lighted candles in one hand and their rosary beads in the other. As they walked, they recited the rosary in Italian, in unison, and with great devotion.

When the procession ended, benediction was given in Italian.

At 7:30 p.m., a gigantic fireworks display was a fitting climax to the pomp and ceremony that had preceded it.

Over the years, the only major change in the celebration has been in the numbers who march and the thousands who come from hundreds of miles to witness this beautiful 91-year-old tradition put on by the grateful citizens of Kenner in honor of their beloved St. Rosalie.

THE MOST UNUSUAL NAUTICAL EXHIBIT
IN THE WORLD
U.S.S. Kidd, Baton Rouge, Louisiana

Whether you have children or not, the U.S.S. Kidd should be a "must" of things to see when in Baton Rouge. The destroyer is named after Rear Admiral Isaac C. Kidd Sr., who was killed aboard his flagship U.S.S. Arizona during the surprise attack at Pearl Harbor.

The U.S.S. Kidd is the only ship now on exhibit in her wartime camouflage paint that caused the ship to blend with the sky above, the horizon and the sea below. The unique dock of the Kidd is the only one of its kind in the world. It allows the ship to be exhibited out of the water when the Mississippi River is in its low stages. Seasonal thaws in the north cause the ship to lift off her unique cradle and float, rising to heights up to 40 feet.

The Kidd has the distinction of holding the record during World War II for rescuing more downed carrier pilots than any other ship. To show exactly what she was made of, during World War II on April 11, 1945, the enemy threw everything it had at the Kidd at Okinawa where the most intense anti-air warfare environment in history took place. On this day, many, many ships were lost along with 5,000 sailors. The U.S.S. Kidd, in spite of receiving a direct hit from a kamikaze attack that killed 38, wounded 50 and inflicted serious damages on the ship, survived, and after receiving necessary repairs, played an important part in the invasion of Japan.

Today, Admiral Isaac C. Kidd Sr., along with his crew, is buried on the flagship Arizona that lies at the bottom of Pearl Harbor.

The U.S.S. Kidd, a gutsy, record holding gallant ship, still in her wartime paint and sitting on a unique cradle on the banks of the mighty Mississippi, anxiously awaits your visit.

TALLY-HO — AMERICA'S OLDEST HUNTING AND FISHING CLUB

The last place on earth one might expect to find the oldest hunting and fishing club in America would be within the city limits of a major city. Yet, the Tally-Ho Club, founded in 1815, is located within the city limits of New Orleans on Chef Menteur Pass.

Prior to the Battle of New Orleans, on the eastern edge of New Orleans, was an area used by professional hunters and fishermen who annually reaped the harvest and supplied the markets of the southern part of the United States with game and fish of every variety. It was virtually a "Sportsman's Paradise," within the city limits.

After the Battle of new Orleans, the area became more accessible when General Andrew Jackson ordered the construction of a military road along Bayous Gentilly and

Sauvage (old Indian trail). The road was to be used in the event the British returned to advance up the "Plains of Gentilly." With construction of this road, the fabulous hunting and fishing area previously inaccessible to New Orleans sportsmen, was now accessible.

In 1815, the Tally-Ho Club was born. To get there from New Orleans you traveled by horse-drawn tally-ho, hence the name of the club was selected. The original building was located on Bayou Sauvage close to Chef Menteur Pass. In 1869, after the railroad from New Orleans to Mobile was completed, the Club built new quarters where it still stands close to the railroad on Chef Menteur Pass.

In 1870, to celebrate the Club's first year in its new quarters, an anniversary dinner was held. In attendance were club members, the Mayor of New Orleans, the Governor of Louisiana, and many other dignitaries. The banquet table offered every imaginable type of food from all parts of the United States, and of course, an ample supply of fresh game and fish from the local area. The table virtually groaned under the weight of the food and drink that was soon to be consumed. The anniversary dinner was so successful it was made an annual event and has been observed every year since.

One of the highlights of the Tally-Ho Club is that it has always maintained good cooks. For one to eat a court bouillion at its hospitality board is enough to make one lick his fingers up to the back of one's neck.

Although fishing year round is very popular, November is the month looked forward to by most members, for this is the time to commence hunting. A wide variety of game over the years has been bagged by the members. In years gone by, many a deer was divided among members and guests of those who went out with the hounds.

The Tally-Ho Club is every bit as active today as it was in years gone by. Some of the club activities include spring and fall

cocktail parties, annual member-guest rodeo, member-son cookout, and annual anniversary dinner.

The Club today has electric lights, running water and air conditioning, but as a reminder of the past, the old gaslight system is still visible. The original iron beds that are collectors' items today are still in use. The Club is also the proud possessor of five original George L. Biabani watercolor paintings and an oil painting of the Club by artist August Noricri, circa 1890. And of great pride, as well as great use, is the ever popular card room.

The Club location makes it vulnerable to hurricanes but no matter how severe the damages, restoration has always been accomplished. A unique design in the main building has been incorporated to prevent the building from floating off its foundation because of storm tides. During rising tides, large floor hatches are opened allowing the rising water into the building. When water recedes, the hatches allow hosing out residual silt. Although the city has extended Eastward for miles during the last 100 plus years, the Tally-Ho Club is still close to thousands of acres of almost virgin marshlands laced by miles of bayous, and dotted with hundreds of ponds and lagoons.

In the evening, after dinner, if a member still hasn't had enough activity during the day, there is a lighted 140-foot boat dock where he can fish while relaxing and sipping on a drink of his choice. That's what you call really living, in America's oldest hunting and fishing club, located within the city limits of New Orleans.

GERMAN SUB SANK IN GULF OF MEXICO
DURING WORLD WAR II

To aid shipping and eliminate the onslaught on American shipping in the Gulf during WWII, a U.S. Coast Guard air base was established in Houma, Louisiana. On August 1, 1942, Chief Aviation Pilot, Henry White and Radioman 1st Class, George "Bo" Boggs, flew out of the Houma air base in a Grumman J-4F-1 Widgeon, an amphibious plane. They had a full load of fuel that gave them little more than four hours flying time. Their mission was to spot and destroy, if possible, German submarines that had been sinking millions of tons of U.S. cargo.

They flew due south over the isles of Dernieres and on to the sunken United Fruit ship buoy. About five minutes later, they cited a submarine 1,500 yards straight ahead of them. The conning tower with the No. U-166 was plainly in sight and her deck was completely exposed. White wanted to pass from stern to bow and drop the bomb directly on top of the sub, but the sub spotted them and started to dive. Thinking quickly, he changed his mind and decided to drop his bomb broadside. White started his dive but had some trouble because the aircraft was not designed for the rigorous flying these Coast Guardsmen were doing. White shouted to Bo, "You will have to release the charge, I am busy with the throttles." At 250 feet, White yelled, "Now," and Bo let her rip. Looking back, they saw a large geyser of water rise from the direct hit. On the climb out of the dive, they spotted a beautiful oil slick. Being low on fuel, they radioed back for assistance and circled the area until another plane arrived from the Houma base. When they landed at the air base, the FBI was waiting to debrief the men. They were sworn to secrecy and did not learn until after the war that they had sunk the only submarine sunk in the Gulf of Mexico or anywhere else by the U.S. Coast Guard during World War II.

This great feat was comparable to scoring a hole in one in golf and not being able to tell anyone.

BATTLE OF NEW ORLEANS

General Andrew Jackson arrived in New Orleans on December 1st, 1814. After surveying the terrain, he took the necessary steps to secure all possible areas of attack. The least likely to be used by the invading army, and the only area believed to give the Americans a chance for victory, was to the east of the city in St. Bernard Parish. On December 8th, one week after Jackson's arrival, the mightiest armada ever to approach American shores was close to the Mississippi delta. The armada consisted of 50 ships with fire power of 1000 guns. Upon learning of this, General Jackson, as a slow-down tactic, sent five gun boats to Lake Borgne to join two ships already there. This was, as one witness explained, like expecting a handful of minnows to block the passage of a whale.

BATTLE OF THE BARGES

The American naval men knew why they were there and were ready and willing to do their duty. They firmly believed

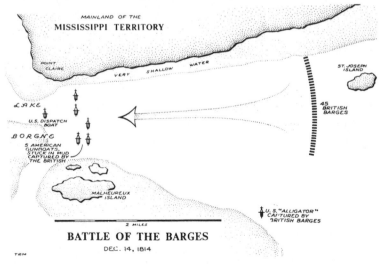

BATTLE OF THE BARGES

DEC. 14, 1814

to a man that they could carry out an effective delaying tactic and give Jackson's forces the necessary time to prepare their defenses against an assault by land. Two hundred and four men on seven ships with twenty-three guns were ready to do whatever was necessary to serve their country. On December 12th, British Admiral Cochrane anchored his command ship at Chandeleur Island. The next day, upon learning that five large cutters armed with six heavy guns each were spotted at the entrance of Lake Borgne, he gave the order to "clear the lake." Cochrane felt that it was impossible to move troops until this flotilla, which he classified as puny, was either captured or destroyed. Without delay, 45 barges carrying 1,500 troops and sailors were on their way. Instead of a unified assault on the Americans, they would pick off the gun boats one by one, like wolves descending on a flock of sheep. Upon seeing the tactics used by the British admiral, American commander, Lieutenant "Tac" Jones, began to fall back. Luck was against him. His vessel ran aground. Should he blow his ship up to keep it out of the enemy's hands or make a suicidal stand? He chose the latter. Jones instructed the masters of the other vessels to inflict as much damage as possible. His instructions to them were to fight until the last man fell. Jones's ship was the first to fall into enemy hands. Jones became a prisoner of war.

On December 14th, seven barges trapped the American ship "Seahorse" against the shore line. What the British didn't know was behind the "Seahorse" was Fort St. Louis. Together the ship and the fort inflicted heavy damages and were successful in driving the British back. The other ships were not as fortunate to have Fort St. Louis behind them. One by one they were boarded. During the next days, hand-to-hand fighting was fierce. The decks were strewn with dead and wounded. As each American vessel was captured, its guns were turned and fired upon another American ship as the American flag flew from the mast of each vessel. It is true the Americans lost this battle, but, when considering their objective was to slow the enemy down to give Jackson time to set up defenses, they were decisive winners. It took nine precious days to clear the lake of what Admiral Cochrane called "a puny flotilla".

Another feather in Jones's cap was the fact his men had shown a stubbornness and skill in battle that was disturbing to the British. The English quartermaster, who witnessed the fighting from a distance, wrote in his journal, "Better shots either with artillery and small arms do not exist than the Americans."

Jones's greatest contribution to the ultimate winning of the Battle of New Orleans was done not at the Battle of the Barges, but the day after. On that day, the British admiral questioned Jones about the Americans' defenses. In a gentlemanly fashion, much appreciated by the admiral, Jones told him of impregnable areas with thousands of troops and heavy fire power, with the plains of Chalmette being the only unprotected area. With this erroneous information, Cochrane chose to land the British troops on the west shore of Lake Borgne. That was the one place of all possible areas of attack where the Americans had a chance to win.

One December 25th, 1814, when General Sir Edward Pakenham, Commander-and-Chief of the British forces, arrived on the battle site selected by the admiral, he was in total shock. The battlefield was narrow, flat and consisted of soft mud. Jackson in a brilliant military move broke the levee and flooded the entire battle field. After the water subsided, British soldiers sank up to their ankles as they walked. On his right flank was a swamp, on his left the river. Enemy guns were on the opposite bank of the river, and a gun boat was able to move up and down the river. Supplies were some forty miles to the rear over rough terrain. If that wasn't bad enough, facing him was a rampart with a canal in front. Worst of all, behind the rampart was an army estimated at 5,400 whose accuracy, as quoted by his quartermaster, "Better shots, either with artillery or small arms, do not exist than Americans."

No doubt, after surveying the situation, the first act performed by General Pakenham on this cold, miserable, rainy Christmas day in 1814, was to sit down and write his last will and testament.

The battle site had been selected and Pakenham had to play the hand that was dealt to him. To do otherwise he would have lost face.

JANUARY 8TH — THE BIG BATTLE

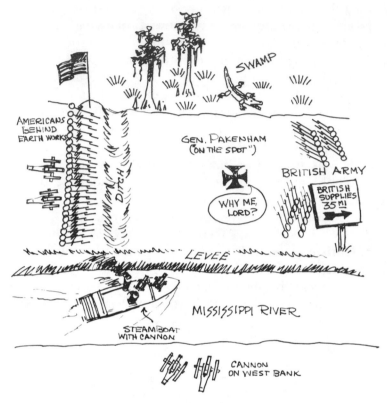

Weather conditions on the day of the battle were foggy with freezing temperatures. Shortly after daylight, when the fog lifted, General Pakenham ordered rockets fired, signaling the start of the attack. British troops, like toy soldiers in a straight line, advanced 60 across and four deep. Jackson gave the order to kill the officers first. It was a virtual massacre. British troops started to retreat. Pakenham watched in stunned disbelief for this had never happened to British soldiers before. He mounted his horse and tried to rally his troops in a charge and was killed instantly.

The accuracy of the American long rifles and the cannon-eers, especially Jean Lafitte's men, was deadly. It was all

over in just 30 minutes. British losses, 3,326 — Americans killed, 13.

As was customary for the times, General Pakenham's heart was removed from his body and buried on the field where he gave his life for his motherland. To preserve his body for return to England, it was placed in a cask of rum.

The Battle of New Orleans was the first major victory of our young country. To this day it's considered our greatest for we won our freedom on July 4, 1776, but it was not confirmed until January 8, 1815, at the Battle of New Orleans.

As a final touch of irony, the battle was fought after the peace treaty (ending the War of 1812) had been signed on December 24, 1814.

Equally ironic is the fact the Battle of New Orleans was not fought in New Orleans, but on the field of Chalmette in St. Bernard Parish.

CHALMETTE MONUMENT
Conceived 1837 — Completed 1909

The Chalmette Monument, if nothing else, is proof that procrastination is not new in Louisiana.

This magnificent monument, though out of proportion, was built to serve as a reminder of one of the greatest military victories in American history. The famous January 8th, 1815, Battle of New Orleans started just before dawn and was for the most part over by noon. It was, to say the least, a very decisive victory.

The building of the monument unfortunately was not as swift or as easy as the battle itself.

In 1839, a group which called itself the Young Men's Jackson

Committee was formed with the intentions of raising the necessary funds to build a monument. A wordy constitution was adopted, but this group proved to be all words and no action. With the death of Andrew Jackson in 1845, interest in the monument was reborn. The name of the new organization was The Jackson Monument Association, and they would be entrusted with the joint project of building not one but two monuments. The first would be in Jackson Square and the other would be on the battlefield itself. This group had more clout than the first and were successful in having the state legislature appropriate $5,000 to acquire a site for the battlefield monument. The Association purchased the land and selected the site of the monument at four arpents (767 feet) from the river along Jackson's old battle line. Now that land had been obtained, the next step was to select a specific design. On May 30, 1855, the Association members examined various plans. The one selected by a unanimous vote was an imposing 150 foot tall Egyptian obelisk. At the base of the monument there would be a series of steps and four Egyptian doorways with only one being functional.

The Association advertised for bids with Richards and Strouds, a Louisiana contractor and only bidder, receiving the contract for $57,000.

By February of 1856, the foundation was completed. It

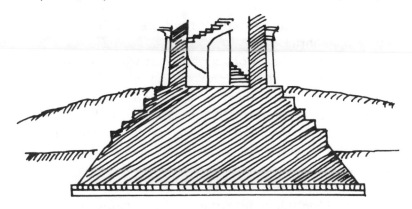

consisted of a series of underlying timbers topped by more than 400,000 bricks.

The first financial problem surfaced when the statue of Jackson ran far above what it was expected to cost leaving the Chalmette Monument short on funds. When construction of the shaft reached 56 feet, 10 inches, far short of the original selected 150 feet, work had to be stopped. To protect the open shaft with the spiral stairway, a temporary wooden pyramidal-shaped roof was installed.

For nearly one-half century the unfinished stump of the Chalmette Monument, now inaccessible because of tall weeds that surround it, stood on the Chalmette plains as a painful reminder of the state's failure to complete it.

In 1888, the State, hoping to get rid of the white elephant, ceded the property to the Federal Government. No doubt the Federal Government was lukewarm on this gift, for other than accepting it, they did nothing to complete it. In 1893, a letter was published in the local newspapers calling attention to the unfinished monument. The next year, the U.S. Daughters of 1776 and 1812 showed an interest and the monument was placed in their care. The State gave the ladies two appropriations of $1,000 each and with the meager revenues derived from the sale of pecans, wood, and rental of the pasture land, they used this money to clear and drain the grounds, place an iron fence across the front, repair old fences, build a mound for the monument, and replace 21 rusty iron steps inside the monument.

In 1896, the ladies felt they were ready to go ahead with the necessary work to complete the monument, but all three bids received were much higher than anticipated. In 1902, the State was asked by the society to request the Federal Government to take over, complete the monument and return it to them. For the next several years no action was taken. Finally in 1907, the Congressional Committee appropriated $25,000. After checking the foundation, it was decided the monument could be increased in height but, to only 100 feet instead of the original 150 feet. It was determined the weight of a 100-foot monument was all the foundation would support. This was unfortunate because the 100 feet makes it out of proportion, because a standard Egyptian obelisk height is 9 to 10 times its width at the base (a true example of the Egyptian obelisk is the Washington Monument).

As the old saying goes, part of a loaf is better than none. Seventy years after the monument idea was born and 54 years after work began, although only 2/3 of the original height, dedication ceremonies were held on March 16, 1909. At the dedication ceremonies the keys to the monument were presented to the U.S. Daughters of 1776 and 1812 in whose care the monument was again entrusted. As though they were playing pingpong, twenty years later, the ladies gave it back to Uncle Sam. They found the work necessary to maintain the monument and the grounds were beyond their capability.

On August 10, 1939, Chalmette was designated a National Historic Park, and from that time on has been a ward of the National Park Service.

COMPARISON

Washington Monument

555 feet high (Tallest Structure In Washington)
Construction took 36 years 5 months 2 days. (1847-1884)
Cost $1,187,710.00

CHAPTER 3

WE NAME OUR TOWNS

LOUISIANA PLACES
STRANGE SOUNDING NAMES

NAMES A TO Z, BUT NEVER AN X

SHORT STORIES OF:

Bunkie

River Ridge

English Turn

Algiers

Lecompte

Westwego

Oaknolia

Pollock

Waterproof

Monroe

LOUISIANA PLACES
STRANGE SOUNDING NAMES

There are today well over 700 cities, towns, villages and hamlets in the State of Louisiana, plus multitudes of communities, with colorful names that are no longer on the map.

Every letter of the alphabet, with the exception of the letter "X", has been used in naming our communities. From Abbeville to Zwolle, the list is long and colorful and like all of Louisiana history, it is entertaining and educational. It does not really matter if you start at the tip of the boot or go to the very top of the state, Louisiana does not have to take a back seat to any other state when it comes to making a statement when naming our towns.

The oldest community in Louisiana is not New Orleans, but Natchitoches. Located in the northwest section of the state, Natchitoches is an Indian word meaning, "chestnut eaters". The community was founded in 1713, five years before New Orleans.

In naming the communities of the state, many different avenues were used. Some of the areas covered were religion, Indian, products of the state, politicians, family names and even a thoroughbred racehorse named Lecomte has a town named in its honor.

Even though Louisiana in many places is below sea level and has no area that could be called mountainous, there are two towns named for height, Mount Airy and Mount Hermon.

Louisiana, before becoming part of the United States, was owned by two Catholic nations, France and Spain. Therefore it is easy to understand why Louisiana has such a heavy sprinkling of saint names for cities and towns. In all, there have been fourteen communities named for saints, from St. Amant to St. Tammany. Of course, if you study Christian writings, you will not find a St. Amant or a St. Tammany. Amant was the family name of the first settlers in that area of the state and St.

Tammany takes its name from a Delaware Indian chief. We also have a Rosaryville, Convent, Red Chruch and Abbeville.

Abbeville was founded because Pere Antoine Desire Megret, pastor of a church in present day Lafayette was at odds with the board of his church. He therefore moved south and built his abbey on a bluff overlooking the Vermillion River. He laid out streets and small farm plots which sold with the provision that buyers pay an annual "interest" to St. Marie Madeleines Chapel. The site of the chapel was originally called, Lachapelle, but the name was changed after a few years to Abbeville.

Louisiana, being blessed with so many rivers and bayous, it was only natural that there would be numerous communities with the prefix bayou before their names. In all, there have been twenty-six, from Bayou Adois to Wauksha. You will also find on the map Ports Sulphur, Eads, Allen and Shreveport as well as a Pilot Town at the mouth of the mighty Mississippi River.

The Indians, having been the first settlers, have certainly left their mark. Mamou is the French equivalent of the Indian word meaning, big hunting ground. Bogalusa means black water; Opelousas, black leg; Pontchatoula, falling hair. And finally, Powhatan, is the translation of the Indian word meaning, hill of the medicine man. There may have been many more Indian names, but Louisiana had one tribe of Indians that practiced cannibalism. These ferocious warriors not only made slaves of their captives, but consumed them as well. These were the Attakapas tribes who were almost annihilated when all the other tribes of the area banned together and tried to eliminate the Attakapas.

Louisiana, with its thriving ports, was a virtual melting pot before the Civil War. Records of the period show that there were sixty-eight different nationalities living within the state's boundaries. The French and Spanish influence is found throughout the state. Also represented are other nations, examples: Caspiana and Sarepta are cities in Russia as well as Louisiana. Copenhagen is the capital city of Denmark and

Louisiana has a city by that name. Sparta and Athens may not be major cities in Louisiana, but they have been major cities in Greece. Alexandria was one of the greatest of cities in Egypt and was truly the heart of their country. Alexandria, Louisiana is located in the heart of the State of Louisiana. Yes, we have a Vienna, Angola, Transylvania and Zwolle was named for a town in Holland. For the Italians we have a Sicily Island, and although Galliano sounds Italian with a vowel on the end, the community is named after a Spaniard, Salvador Galiano. Unfortunately his name was misspelled when the maps were made. Independence, Louisiana is often called Little Italy because of the large Italian population.

Louisiana has towns named French Settlement and Germantown (DesAllemands). Spanish Governor, Bernardo de Galvez, sent colonists to southwest Louisiana and gave each family five arpents of land, fronting a stream and extending as far back from it as a man could clear the land. Each family was also given an ax, sickle, spade, hoe, two hens and a rooster, two pigs and enough food for the first years. In appreciation the settlers named the community New Iberia after the ancient name of Spain. Of course French general Lafayette was the number one hero of the French people living in Louisiana, so they changed the name of Vermillion City to Lafayette. And let's not forget Napoleon, "ville."

There is, of course, humor to be found everywhere. The naming of some of our cities is no exception. To start off with, we do have a town called Aloha. It is so small, it is jokingly said, the same sign says hello and goodby. Bethany, Louisiana was originally called, "Lick of the Skillet." Other unusual names include Uneedus, Dry Prong, Waterproof, Jigger and Cut Off. We have a Pleasant Hill and a Slaughter. There is Solitude and Ball, Champagne, Welcome and Relief, Retreat and Paradise, Enterprise and Pride. Since Louisiana is located deep in the South, it was only fitting that there be a town called Dixie. The state bird is the pelican and a town of that name we do have. With the wealth of Louisiana's gas, oil and seafood industry, we could be an empire all by ourselves and therefore we do have an Empire, Louisiana on our map. Lumber has always been a big industry in Louisiana with the largest sawmill in the world, The Great Southern Lumber Company, located in Bogalusa, Louisiana for thirty years. Yes, we do have a community named, Trees. Fishing and hunting has always been tops in the state. Our license plate proudly proclaimed Louisiana as "Sportsman's Paradise." Cotton was the product responsible for Louisiana having more millionaires than any other state before the Civil War. It is only fitting we have a town named Cottonport. Sugar is what sweetened the economy and as a reminder, Sugartown. Red beans without rice would be unthinkable. To eliminate that dilemma, there was at one time a town named Riceville. At the tip of the Louisiana boot in St. Bernard and Plaquemine parishes are grown naval oranges that are as sweet as any to be found on the face of the earth. And rightfully so, we have a community called Orange Grove.

Oil, called by some Black Gold, has been an economic blessing to our state and to go without an Oil City would be blasphemous. Today there are more Creoles living in Louisiana than any other state, it is only natural that we have a town named Creole.

It is surprising to find as many men's first names as female names. Some male names are Archie, Maurice, Scott, Edgar, Matthew, Robert, Douglas, Walker, Oscar, Vernon, Mitchell, Terry, Gilbert, Taylor and Floyd. Female names range from Angie, Lucy, Ida, Elizabeth, Effie, Rosa, Ruby, Luella, Bernice, Cecile, Joyce, Ethel, Lily, Irene and Lottie.

There are cities named after pirates as well as politicians. Some people who have lived in Louisiana for a long time are convinced there is little or no difference in the two. Lafitte, Louisiana is named in honor of the famous pirate, Jean Lafitte, who helped save the city of New Orleans from the British attack. Great men like Destrehan, Poydras and Belle Chasse (also misspelled), are remembered with towns named in their honor. Each of the three served in a capacity in state government that would be equivalent to today's lieutenant governor. Slidell, Louisiana is named after John Slidell, a very powerful Louisiana political leader who served in the state senate and who was called the political boss of the state during the 1850s. He was later appointed minister of Mexico by the President of the United States. On the national political scene we have the towns of Washington and Vernon. They were named for the first president of the United States and his home town, Mount Vernon. Although Taft was President of the United States, Taft, Louisiana was named for his brother who had a lumber interest in Louisiana.

NAMES — A - Z — BUT NEVER AN X

Ajax

The two men most responsible for naming the town owned a cotton gin and a saw mill. Both were run with Ajax engines that were truly flawless in operation, therefore the name of the town — Ajax.

Breaux Bridge

In the early history of southwest Louisiana the inhabitants of present day Breaux Bridge were required to cross Bayou Teche on a toll ferry. Agricole Breaux built a toll-free bridge and the settlement took the name Breaux's Bridge.

Carencro

Carencro is the French designation for the turkey buzzard. The area was inundated with turkey buzzards, hence the name Carencro.

Echo

The name Echo was given by a steamboat captain. When arriving at their destination the captains blew their whistles as they approached the landing. When they did, the sound would echo back from the woods. What better name for the community than Echo.

ances Folsom

Folsom

Two brothers named Fendleson were the first settlers in the area. Grover Cleveland was President at the time. The brothers were great admirers of this eminent statesman. Cleveland had just married Miss Frances Folsom, the Fendlesons named the village after her.

George

Georgetown

Georgetown is possibly the only settlement in the United States that is named for a hobo. One day in the small community a hobo showed up out of the blue. He worked hard, was well liked and even respected by many. When a car of lumber had to be shipped it required a name, so by general acclamation the name Georgetown was selected. Like any good hobo, George moved on to unknown territory, but the town still carries his name.

Michael Hahn

Hahnville
Named for Michael Hahn, a newspaper publisher, plantation owner, U.S. Congressman and Governor of Louisiana in 1864 — who resigned as Governor of Louisiana after only one year.

Ida
Jonathan R. Chandler named the town after his second daughter, Ida.

"NAME IT FOR ME, DADDY."

Jigger

The postmaster of the community, at the request of the U.S. Post Office, was compiling a list of possible names for the town. His five-year-old son suggested he list his name, Jigger. Jigger was the United States Post Office choice.

Kurthwood

Mr. J.H. Kurth was the founder of a large lumber mill. He named the town using his family name and the product of his business, therefore the name Kurthwood.

Lismore

A good Irishman named O'Rourk, settled in Concordia Parish. He was from Lismore, a small town on the Black River in Ireland. He named the Louisiana town Lismore in memory of his hometown in Ireland. Lismore, Louisiana is ironically also located on Black River.

Mamou

Mamou is an Indian word meaning, "big hunting ground". The name suits the area for it is truly a hunter's paradise.

Norco
    Stands for New Orleans Refining Company.

Oil City
    The first oil and gas discovered in Louisiana was in 1870. A city was born and took the name Oil City.

Panola
    Choctaw word for cotton.

Quitman
    Named for Mr. Quitman Brooks, its founder and first postmaster.

Reserve

Leon Goudechaux, as a young man worked up and down the river as a salesman. It was his custom to spend the night on any plantation where night overtook him. One night he applied for lodging at the Soubenir Plantation owned by Antione Boudousqui. Leon was shocked when he was refused accommodation. He said to himself, "I will forgive, but I will not forget. One day I will 'reserve' this plantation for myself." In 1850 his promise came to pass. The Soubenir Plantation had to be sold and Goudechaux bought it and renamed it Reserve. The town took the same name.

St. Francisville

In 1738 a Capuchin priest was authorized to build a chapel on the west bank of the river in Point Coupee Parish. The name St. Francis of Assisi, the patron saint of the Capuchins was selected. When death occurred on the lowlands, the bodies were boated across the river to the highlands on the east and buried in consecrated ground. When a village was finally established on the east bank, the people selected the name St. Francisville.

Triumph
    After Ft. Jackson was defeated and occupied during the Civil War, the name Triumph was given as a reminder of the event by the unwelcome Yankee visitors.

Uneedus
    In this farming community, the owners of Lake Superior Piling Company used the slogan "you need us". It was so successful the town was named for the slogan.

Venice
    The name was a very easy one for the people to select. Like Venice, Italy, the city is surrounded by miles and miles of canals.

Welcome

The most prominent business in the area was a sugar plantation originally name Webre Plantation. When it changed hands it was renamed Bon Secour — French for welcome. When a town was established it was named Bon Secour, but changed at a later date to the English equivalent — Welcome.

X

There has never been a town in Louisiana starting with the letter X.

Youngsville

This community was originally named Royville. Since much confusion existed at the post office because there was a town in north Louisiana named Rayville, Royville changed its name to Youngsville for one of the early beloved doctors named Young.

"I will name this place Zwolle, after my hometown."

Zwolle

A Dutchman named Jan De Goeijen named the town after his hometown in Holland.

SHORT STORIES OF NAMING OF
LOUISIANA CITIES

1. BUNKIE
2. RIVER RIDGE
3. ENGLISH TURN
4. ALGIERS
5. LECOMPTE
6. WESTWEGO
7. OAKNOLIA
8. POLLOCK
9. WATERPROOF
10. MONROE

BUNKIE

On the map of Louisiana you will find many cities with unique colorful and even humorous names. There are, of course, a few simple names like Jones and Iowa, but on the whole, most of the names are colorful as well as have interesting stories as to how they were derived.

Bunkie, located in central Louisiana approximately 30 miles south of Alexandria, is a combination of unique, colorful and humorous. It is far from plain and simple and has an

interesting story as to how it came about. Captain Samuel Haas, a Civil War veteran, became a successful businessman and landowner after the war. In the course of pursuing his business interest he traveled extensively. Each time he returned from a business trip he brought his young daughter a gift, usually a toy. Upon returning from one of his many trips he brought her a very popular toy of the day. It consisted of two wooden sticks approximately six to eight inches long. At the top of each stick a string connected the two ends. Suspended from the string was a little thin multi jointed wooden monkey. When the bottom of the two sticks was squeezed the monkey would swing around. When she squeezed the sticks her little

"Bunkie" swung around. Monkey was just not in her young vocabulary.

When the railroad came through the area Captain Haas donated the necessary land for a new town. He was advised in appreciation of his great gift he would have the honor of naming the town anything he wished. Everyone thought he would choose his family name. He fooled them all. He chose instead the name "Bunkie" in honor of his little daughter, and Bunkie it has been ever since.

LITTLE FARMS, RIVER RIDGE, SAUVE, OR CLANCY

Communities derive their names in many different ways. Some take the names of their founding fathers or families, others from previous inhabitants such as Indian names. There are those whose names are derived from particular happenings: example, the flooding of the Mississippi River led to the names, Dry Prong and Waterproof. Very few communities however, have a chance to choose their own names.

Until 1974, the River Ridge area, even though located in Jefferson Parish, was known for mailing purposes as "New Orleans, 21", later "New Orleans, 23", and after the zip codes came into existence, "New Orleans, 70123". Many people referred to the area as Little Farms for the subdivision of that name.

On January 11, 1974, Postmaster Paul V. Burke sent a letter to residents of the area advising them that New Orleans would be deleted from their address and their new official address would be Harahan, Louisiana 70123. The reason given for the change was to avoid clerical errors and misunderstandings resulting in tax revenues being given to Orleans Parish instead of Jefferson Parish.

This letter triggered a group of citizens from the various subdivisions affected to ask the Parish Council on January 31, 1974, to allow them to select the name of their choice since it was their community. A committee was chosen, and the wheels were put into motion to select a new name. On March 7, 1974, three names were presented —Little Farms, River Ridge and Sauve. At this meeting a group came forward and suggested that the name "Clancy" (a previous sheriff of the parish) be added to the other three names. This caused a multitude of recommendations. To satisfy the people of the area, the ballot was sent out to every resident landowner with the following names (in addition to Little Farms, River Ridge and Sauve).

Bellegarde	Highland Farms	River Farms
Bourg Orleans	Hyland Farms	Riverland
Breckenridge	Just	River Point Cannes
Brulees	Lafreniere	River Road
Clancy	La Providence	Riverside
Delachaise	Le Jeffersonion	Riverside Park
Eastwego	Levee	Riverwood
Elmwood	Metairie Ridge	Riverwoods
Elmwood Park	Moss Ridge	Rural
Elmwood Ridge	Mosswood	Sauve Heights
Elmwood View	Moss Woods	Sauve Point
Faubourg Orleans	Oak Alley	Sauve Ridge Forest
Ridge	Pierre Sauve	Shangrila
Frenchman	Providence	Taint
Hazel Farms	Redgate	Terre Sauve
Highgate	Redgate Farms	Upstream
High Point	Ridgewood	Woodridge Highland
Acres	River Bend	
		_____
		Write in Name

When all ballots were counted, Little Farms received the largest number with 1,170. River Ridge was second with 877, and Sauve received 226. Although the name Clancy caused all the ruckus, it received only 16 votes, just twice as many as the recommendation of write in Kate.

A run-off election was held between the two front runners. Even though Little Farms had won on March 7th, in the final election, River Ridge received 1,645 votes, becoming the winner, with Little Farms receiving 1,485.

On June 6, 1974 the Jefferson Parish Council, in resolution 23886, officially designated "That the unincorporated area of the Parish of Jefferson comprising Zip Code No. 70123, shall hereafter be designated and officially known as River Ridge, Louisiana 70123."

ENGLISH TURN

This year for the first time, the USF&G Golf Tournament was played on the all new Jack Nicholas English Turn Golf Course. The name "English Turn," although new to the millions who watched on TV as well as those involved in the tournament, is far from being new. English Turn is one of the oldest names to be found on the early maps of Louisiana.

The story behind the name is as follows: In 1698, Pierre Le Moyne Sieur d'Iberville led an expedition to find the mouth of the Mississippi River. On March 2, 1699, he located and entered the mouth of the river and slowly ventured up-stream. Near the mouth of the Red River, his party turned around and headed back towards the Gulf of Mexico. Iberville sent his little brother, Bienville, down river the same way they came. He returned to the Gulf by way of Bayou Manchac, for the Indians told him it was much faster (Manchac means back entrance). At the great bend of the river just below the present site of New

Orleans, Bienville encountered an English ship. He told the captain who he was, and emphasized that his brother, Iberville, was upstream with a great warship. He fibbed. He also advised there was a small detachment of a large French force also stationed upstream. This was also untrue. Iberville, the French naval genius, was highly respected by the English. He had never been on the losing side of a marine battle with the mighty English. With this in mind, the captain quickly turned his ship around and went back into the Gulf of Mexico. The spot where this incident occurred was appropriately named "English Turn," and remains so to this day.

ALGIERS

In New Orleans, in the early days of the present-day French Quarter, all buildings were made of wood including the roofs. Each building butted against the next, streets were very narrow, and there was no professional fire department. As a fire precaution, an ordinance was passed stating that all powdered ammunition had to be stored in a magazine built for that purpose on the west bank of the Mississippi River.

Two French soldiers who had just been transferred to Louisiana from the town of Algiers, in Algeria, North Africa, were assigned to guard the powder magazine. One said to the other, "My God, it's like we are still in Algiers." The descriptive word used by the soldier was from then on used to describe the area.

The name Algiers is the phonetic rendering of the Arabic words meaning, "the islet", "the island" or "peninsula." There is a certain similarity between the two Algiers in this respect. Algiers, Louisiana, is an island in the sense that it is encircled by swamp, except where it borders the Mississippi River. Furthermore, while Algiers in North Africa lies across the Mediterranean from the erstwhile "parent" France, Algiers in Louisiana is situated across the Mississippi River from its "parent" New Orleans.

Algiers was annexed as part of New Orleans on March 14, 1870.

LECOMPTE

On April 1, 1854, a memorable horse race was held at the famous Metairie Course. The race, advertised as "The Great State Post Stakes," became a state rivalry between Louisiana and Kentucky. Although there were four horses from four southern states, the Louisiana and Kentucky horses were on the lips and the tips of the pens of writers throughout the U.S.

The Louisiana-bred entry was Lecomte, from the stables of Thomas J. Wells, owner of a plantation near Alexandria. Representing Kentucky was a horse named Lexington. Everyone who was anyone was on hand for this great event – governors, mayors, and congressmen from numerous states, business and professional elite, along with none other than U.S. President Millard Filmore, who stated, "There is no way I would miss this great sporting event."

A match race in those days was a grueling test of speed and endurance in four-mile heats, with the winner being the horse with the best time in the three runnings. On this particular day, the track was muddy, and Lexington's victory was considered by many a freak. As stated — the horse was a lucky "mudder". A rematch was demanded. This time Lecomte was not only the winner, but won in record time. Again there were calls for a rematch. On April 14, 1855, Tom Wells, owner of Lecomte, challenged Lexington in a head-to-head "rubber" match, with the winner being awarded $20,000. This time there was no question; Lexington was declared the winner, with a time of 7:23 - 3/4. When it was all over, it was heard in the crowd, "Besides the $20,000 purse, there were surely some plantations that changed hands today."

The race of April 14, 1855, was the last for both horses. They both gave great enjoyment to many when they competed. Even though it is over a hundred and thirty years since their last race, they are both still remembered. Lexington's skeleton can be seen today properly mounted in the Smithsonian Institute, Washington, D.C. Lecomte is remembered through a town located south of Alexandria that was named in his honor, even though the name was misspelled — LECOMPTE.

WESTWEGO

Have you ever considered the fact that, broken down, the name of Westwego is the only city in Louisiana, and possibly any other state, that is a complete sentence. Also interesting is the fact that there is not only one but two stories on how the city got its name.

Story number one: Before the opening of the Huey P. Long Bridge, all trains crossed the river on ferry boats. When they got to the other side, each car was marked with chalk with the direction it had to go. The markings "west we go" were on the vast majority; therefore, the town took the name Westwego.

Story number two: People living along the coastline of Louisiana, after being struck on numerous occasions by storms, were directly hit in 1893 by a severe, devastating storm and decided that enough was enough. They walked in-land. Upon reaching the Mississippi River, they moved up river until ending their journey at this location and said, "This is as far west as we will go." Hence the name Westwego.

As to which story is the correct one — your guess is as good as anyone's.

One thing we do know, before the present name was adopted, the town was called Salaville for Pablo Sala, the man who donated a plot of ground to each of the families who had been displaced by the hurricane. After this generous gesture, it doesn't seem fair his name was rejected in favor of the name Westwego.

OAKNOLIA
(No Longer on the Map)

Sometimes, when you can't have exactly what you want, it is necessary to compromise. As the old saying goes, "A half loaf is better than none." The town of Oaknolia was just such a case. In the southern part of East Feliciana Parish in 1911 (nine miles west of present-day Slaughter), the citizens made plans to apply for a name for their new town. At first, they thought Magnolia would be appropriate, because the area was prolific with magnolia trees. But, unfortunately, the name Magnolia

had already been taken. The citizens put their creative thinking caps back on. In a short time, they realized there were also beautiful oak trees in the area. It was decided to combine the two names, substituting "oak" for "mag". Hence, the unusual name Oaknolia.

Someone must have forgotten to water Oaknolia, for it has withered away and is no longer on the Louisiana map.

POLLOCK

If you were to ask 100 dyed-in-the wool true blooded Americans who Oliver Pollock was, chances are in unison they would answer, "Oliver who!" Yet, his $370,000 contribution to the American cause of freedom was the single largest financial contribution received by these desperate Americans.

He was a super-duper New Orleans salesman and with 300 to 400 boats trading on the rivers of North America, plus ships traveling to every major port in the world, he was one of the wealthiest men in North America.

Oliver Pollock

Pollock freely gave not only money but much needed supplies to the Americans who were fighting for their freedom. Besides his financial support, his super-duper salesmanship convinced the Spanish, under the able leadership of Governor Galvez, to aid the American cause by driving the English out of Baton Rouge, Natchez, Mobile and Pensacola. When Pollock's finances ran out, he pledged his credit to the limit with the

Spanish authorities to furnish the Americans additional, urgently needed supplies. When the fighting was over and freedom secured, Pollock hurried to Philadelphia for some assistance as his creditors were hot on his heels. He received a very cool reception from Congress. They, no doubt too, said, Oliver who! To improve his financial situation, he went on a business trip to Cuba where he was instantly thrown into jail for 18 months by the Spanish authorities. Luckily, his old friend, Galvez, found out about his situation and bailed him out to the tune of $151,693. Pollock made a gentlemen's agreement to pay the sum back. He also persuaded one of his loyal employees to stay in jail in his place until the sum was paid, (we said he was a super salesman) which he did.

In spite of the shabby treatment he received from Congress, on October 10, 1786, 10 years after America's independence, he was proud to stand and receive his American citizenship.

It just seems that the American government, for one reason or another, had it in for Oliver Pollock as he has received very little recognition in our history books, and the only two portraits ever painted of this man were destroyed during the Civil War by the United States federal gunboat Essex.

Today, the only physical remembrance of the great man from Louisiana who did so much to help the Americans win their freedom is a plaque in the 400 block of Chartres Street, in New Orleans, where he once lived and a town in central Louisiana named in his honor.

WATERPROOF

In the 1830s, pioneers settled on the banks of the Mississippi River on the Louisiana side just north of present-day Natchez, Mississippi. The location was a popular spot for covered wagons on their way to Texas. As many as fifty covered wagons made the crossing in one day at this strategic location. Many of the settlers, tired by their long journeys and attracted by the fertility of the soil, once they crossed the river to the Louisiana side, unhitched their wagons and made this area their homes.

On numerous occasions, the area was completely under many feet of water. On one such occasion, Abner Smalley, one of the earlier settlers, was standing high and dry on a small strip of land surrounded by water as far as the eye could see. He was waiting for a steamboat to land for its usual refueling of cord wood. As the boat came in to land, the jovial captain took in the scene, then called out to Mr. Smalley, "Well, Abner, I see you're waterproof." With this, the name of the town was born. Although the name Waterproof remains the same, the location is 2 1/2 miles from its original location. The reason — banks of the river continued caving until 1880. Since that time, because of bigger and better levees, the town of Waterproof has been just that — waterproof.

MONROE

Many ships have been named after cities, but Monroe was the only city to be named after a ship. The Ouachita River, like the Mississippi River, has a very strong current. In 1819, four hundred citizens and a detachment of military personnel were stationed at Fort Miro, located on the Ouachita River. Everyone was full of excitement when they saw the steamboat James Monroe belching thick black smoke as she came steaming up the Ouachita River. Captain J. A. Paulfrey, was the first to venture on this mighty river in a steamboat. Until the vessel James Monroe arrived, the area of Ft. Miro was called Prairie des Camois (Prairie of Canoes), because it served as a point of departure for traders and trappers taking their wares down the river to New Orleans.

The steamboat Monroe proved river traffic would soon be coming up and down the river and with it unbound prosperity. With this in mind, the citizens from Ft. Miro, headed by Henry Bry, went on board the James Monroe and with great enthusiasm shook the hand of Captain Paulfrey and thanked him repeatedly.

Because Captain Paulfrey had conquered the mighty Ouachita River, and, because of what was destined financially for the area, it was decided that to show their appreciation, the community should be named Monroe in recognition of the steamship James Monroe.

Upon reflection, although the town was named for the steamboat, the steamboat in retrospect was named for James Monroe, a key figure in the Louisiana Purchase and at the time President of the United States. The name Monroe showed the desire for a new start under a new flag and a patriotic gesture of the people of this new government.

CHAPTER 4

PLANTATIONS

DEFINITION

WEDDING OF WEDDINGS

NOTTOWAY

LE PETITE VERSAILLES

ETIENNE DE BORE

MARIGNY PLANTATION BELL

GHOST

EMBELLISHMENTS

1. Double Curving Stairways
3. One Of A Kind
4. Ivory Buttons
5. Cooling System At Dinner
6. Slave Quarters
7. King's Throne
8. Where Are The Closets
9. Pigeonniers
10. Draperies Made A Statement

1990 LOUISIANA PLANTATIONS

DEFINITION:

PLANTATION

Large estate usually worked by resident labor, a place that is planted or under cultivation.

From the very simple to the ultra-magnificent, plantations were located and are still found in every area of the state. After 200 years, many of these plantations are not only still standing, but in many instances are used as family homes. Others serve only as tourist attractions. Through sheer neglect some are run-down beyond repair. Others, through care and a deep desire to preserve our past, have been restored to their original splendor.

The majority of plantations were and still are located on rivers, bayous or other waterways. The reason being, water was the principal means of transportation when they were built. Roads, until the coming of the automobile in the early 20th century, were almost nonexistant. When built, the plantations were set back away from the waterways. Rows of trees, in some cases each named for a member of the family, were planted on both sides of a road or walkway making for a shady approach from the waterway to the front door of the plantation.

A WEDDING OF WEDDINGS

Charles Durande, a prosperous aristocrat from France, arrived in Louisiana shortly after the War of 1812. He immediately established himself on the banks of Bayou Teche, near the town of St. Martinville. From the start his sugar plantation was very successful. Prior to that unpleasantness called the Civil War, he was among the wealthiest of prosperous Louisiana planters. Durande did everything on a grand scale. His palatial brick and cypress plantation home, which was surrounded by thousands of acres of rich land he owned, was reached by an alleyway 1-1/4 miles long of alternating oak and pine trees that were planted by his small army of slaves. He called this luscious area of green, "Pine Alley". Upon his awakening each morning, the doors of his mansion were thrown open and all its rooms sprayed with perfume. He and his entire family bathed in cologne water. His carriage was ostentatiously upholstered with cloth of gold. He was rich in slaves, land and gold, but much richer in progeny. He was married twice, each wife bearing him 12 children.

Of all his grandiose ideas, he outdid himself when two of his daughters from his second wife, having both reached a proper age for finding proper suitors, announced at the same time that they were to be married, each to a prominent St. Martinville family.

Durande gave this important event great thought. He would

prepare a wedding celebration that even a princess of his native France might well have envied.

For this all-important function, Durande ordered from Cathay, China, a strange cargo. It consisted of thousands upon thousands of huge live spiders which he had freed in the tall trees of Pine Alley. In no time, the spiders spun clouds of huge webs among the branches from one end of the long alley to the other. Once this was done, the broad roadway beneath the alley was covered with heavy, rich, bright-colored carpets. On each side of the long alley, hundreds of tables were covered with food, wine, and floral arrangements. All were lighted and highlighted by thousands of huge candles. If front of the mansion, a magnificent altar was erected. Two thousand guests, consisting of prominent planters, as well as townspeople small and great, were invited to attend this once-in-a-lifetime happening.

Early in the morning of the day of the wedding, slaves climbed into the trees and installed the crowning glory of the event. Durande had ordered great quantities of gold and silver dust, which the slaves sprinkled on the dew-covered spider webs. At dusk, all 2,000 guests, each with a front-row view, stood in awe as the candlelight illuminated the gold and silver spider webs as the bridal procession marched the entire length of the alley.

This unbelievable event was the most ingenious function

conceived of and carried out in the lavish life of Charles Durande.

Just as the breathtaking sight of the silver and gold spider webs glittering in the lights of the flickering candles as the brides and their bridal parties walked under Pine Alley was embedded in the minds of all 2,000 guests for the rest of their lives, so, too, will this legend continue to live for our generation and many generations to come.

NOTTOWAY PLANTATION — THE LARGEST PLANTATION HOME IN THE SOUTH

Before the Civil War, because of the extremely healthy economic conditions, Louisiana had more millionaires than any other state and therefore was blessed with more than its share of palatial ante-bellum homes.

Because of the devastation in Louisiana during the Civil War, plus the march of progress through construction of chemical, petrochemical and other industrial plants on the rivers of Louisiana, many of the plantation homes of the past can only be seen in books.

Nottoway Plantation in White Castle, Louisiana dodged both the devastation of the war and progress and today stands as a living monument of how successful people lived before the Civil War.

In 1857, John Hampden Randolph, originally from Virginia and a highly successful sugarcane planter, commissioned Henry Howard, one of New Orleans' most successful architects, to design and supervise construction of a three story mansion. He insisted that there be at least 365 openings, a large ballroom suitable to marry off his many daughters, and lastly that there be no knots in the timbers used in construction of the home.

The design of the 53,000 square foot plantation, with 22

enormous columns surrounding the building, was a blend of Greek Revival and Italianate.

There were 200 windows and 165 doors fulfilling the request of an opening for each day of the year. Inside the home, elegance was everywhere. Crystal chandeliers, hand carved marble mantels, music conservatory and a few features that were well ahead of their time in the form of wall to wall carpeting and hot and cold running water.

To fill the second request, Howard designed an elegant, breathtaking ballroom that was white from the enameled white floors to the pure white plastered ceiling. To divide the large room he used hand carved cypress Corinthian column archways. Even though the room was enormous he added one more innovation. The windows leading to the circular porch were designed to lift out of the way so dancers could go from ballroom to porch and back into the ballroom.

As stated in the contract, there would be no knots in the lumber. As the slaves cut the timbers they sang to keep rhythm. As they repeatedly came across knots they sang "knot away."

When Mr. Randolph came to inspect the building's progress he would hear the slaves singing repeatedly "knot away" and decided he would name his new home Nottoway, the same as the county name he came from in Virginia.

LE PETITE VERSAILLES

Gabriel Valcour Aime, known as "Louis XIV of Louisiana," was a highly-successful businessman. He owned a working plantation that included a vast agricultural experimental station. It was located on the West Bank of the Mississippi River twenty miles south of Donaldsonville. The plantation was referred to as "Le Petit Versailles."

When building his palatial plantation home in 1799, Valcour Aime used the traditional Louisiana style of architecture with eight massive columns. The one difference, it had wings on each side that extended backward, enclosing a Spanish style patio. It was as plush as any plantation home in Louisiana. The floors and stairs were all made of Italian marble. Valcour Aime also had hidden stairs built into the thick walls, allowing him to get around from room to room without anyone knowing his whereabouts.

As beautiful as his home was, the highlights of his plantation were the gardens and hot houses. The gardens were far from being ordinary. To be sure they were not ordinary, Valcour Aime brought to Louisiana the French horticulturist responsible for upkeep of the gardens at the Versailles Palace in France. To adequately supply his gardens, he built hot houses where he raised and cultivated flowers, trees and shrubs from all four corners of the earth. When everything was in bloom, it was a breathtaking sight. In one of the hot houses, by being able to control the climate, he was able to grow food products that were not indigenous to the area.

When Louis Philippe, future king of France, visited Le Petit Versailles, he was greeted, as he approached by water, by cannon fire from the small fort built on the river for just such welcome of special guests. The fort also served for the playful enjoyment of his beloved children. After Valcour Aime and Louis dined, the gold plates they had used for their meal were thrown in the river. This gesture was synonymous of Rex toasting his Mardi Gras Queen, and then breaking the glass.

Valcour Aime, in spite of all of his wealth, was not of a braggadocio or ostentatious nature. One evening, while dining with a friend who was every bit the gourmet as himself, the two men spoke of the outstanding greatness of their chefs. Valcour Aime's friend told of how his chef would go to distant markets to acquire the necessary ingredients to prepare what he considered a perfect meal. Valcour Aime said to his friend, "If you will be my guest at my home in St. James, I will promise you a dinner that you yourself will admit is perfect, every item of which will come from my own plantation." "Impossible," said the New Orleans epicure, "I do not doubt, my friend, that you can supply most of a dinner from your land, but a perfect dinner from your own plantation, that is impossible." "Do you care to wager that it is impossible," asked Valcour Aime, "and you yourself on your own word of honor to be the judge?" "Ten thousand dollars," said the New Orleans man. "It is a bet," said Valcour Aime.

The dinner was eaten in the great dining hall in St. James. There were terrapins, shrimp, crabs, snipes, quail, breast of wild duck, vegetables, salads, fruits, coffee, cigars, wines and liqueurs at the end.

"What say you, my friend?" questioned Valcour Aime. "The dinner is perfect, but I think you lose," answered the epicure.

"For no man can supply me with bananas, coffee, and tobacco grown in St. James, Valcour Aime."

"Ah, my friend, wait a moment," said Valcour Aime. He ordered horses, slaves and lanterns. They mounted and rode to a glass enclosed conservatory containing plots of coffee, tobacco, bananas and pineapples.

As stated, Valcour Aime was not of a braggadocio nature; he was not bragging but simply stating a fact. Upon completion of the meal, his guest acknowledged that he did have a perfect meal with all products coming from the plantation, making Valcour Aime $10,000 richer. One can only wonder if his friend added fifteen percent as a tip for good service.

Unfortunately, in 1920, disaster struck. Historical Le Petit Versailles plantation home caught fire and burned to the ground. The only structure on the vast plantation still remaining, but in almost unrecognizable condition, is the little fort built for the welcome of visitors, including the future King of France, and the enjoyment of Valcour Aime's children.

ETIENNE DeBORE PLANTATION
16TH CENTURY SUCCESS STORY

Etienne DeBore, New Orleans' first appointed mayor, was world renowned, not for his achievements as mayor, but for being the first man in history to successfully granulate sugar commercially. DeBore's huge, fertile plantation was located up river from New Orleans. It occupied all of what is now Audubon Park, Tulane and Loyola Universities and adjacent lands. In 1797, DeBore took a huge gamble by planting sugar cane on his entire plot of ground. Sugar had never before been

granulated on a commercial scale. His friends told him he was flirting with disaster. No one in the world had ever achieved what he proposed to do. Some said no one in his right mind would attempt what DeBore proposed. Some friends even implied that DeBore might be smoking some of those funny weeds. DeBore's gamble paid off. He did what he said he would do and in doing so became world famous, not to mention very wealthy.

In 1803, when Louisiana Governor William C.C. Claiborne was looking for a mayor for New Orleans, the shining star of DeBore's achievements made him a likely candidate.

Just as DeBore became world renowned for his achievements, his grandson, Charles Gayarre became equally renowned in Louisiana. He was the state's first historian. His four-volume history of Louisiana is one of the bibles of Louisiana history.

When Tulane University built a football stadium, it was eventually labeled "THE SUGAR BOWL". Apropos, wouldn't you say? It was on this very ground that the stadium occupied that sugar was successfully granulated commercially for the first time in history. The iron pot in which this great achievement was performed is in Baton Rouge, on the LSU campus next to, what else, the LSU experimental sugar foundry.

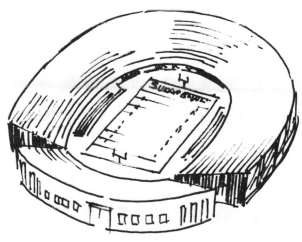

MARIGNY PLANTATION

Bernard Mandeville de Marigny, one of the wealthiest men in all of North America in the 1700s, had a plantation on the north shore of Lake Pontchartrain (now Mandeville, Louisiana). Bernard, with his vast wealth, was willing to go to any financial means to be sure he was afforded all the conveniences available to him. He traveled frequently between his plantation and his palatial home in New Orleans. He devised the following ingenious method to be sure his carriage was awaiting him upon his arrival on the south shore: he had a massive bell cast that was to be rung when he prepared to leave his plantation. To make certain the bell would ring as clearly as man could make it, he furnished $10,000 in silver coins to the foundry that cast the bell. The coins were melted down and added to the molten metal when it was ready to be poured. The financial investment paid off, and Bernard achieved his goal. When rung, the sound was so clear and piercing that it traveled all the way across the 24-mile-wide lake and could be heard by his staff on the south shore.

As the old saying goes, "If you've got it, flaunt it," and old Bernard Mandeville de Marigny had a multitude of ways of doing just that.

GHOSTS

Throughout Louisiana, plantations vary in many ways, from size and design, to specific crops, from simplicity to elegance beyond imagination.

The differences are numerous and equally noticeable upon inspection. One common thread, even though you are not able to see it, or them if that is the case, are ghosts. This writer has never ever visited a plantation or read of a specific plantation where there was not an interesting, attention getting, story of a ghost on the property. Any plantation worth its salt had a series of ghosts. If they had only one, they did not even mention it for fear of shame.

The Cottage, located on River Road just south of Baton Rouge was built by Frederick E. Conrad in 1830. Mr. Conrad had a very close friend named Holt. During the Civil War both men were captured and imprisoned by Union forces. After the war they were released and went back to live at the Cottage. Conrad died shortly after returning. Holt, on the other hand, continued to live on the plantation for many, many years. When Holt finally died, he was buried on the plantation grounds. It wasn't long after his death reports by a number of different people were made claiming to have seen him wondering around the house. Sightings of Mr. Holt were made for many, many years. Who knows, maybe he was looking for the key to the front door of the Cottage, or for his old friend Frederick E. Conrad.

The Kenelworth Plantation just below New Orleans, boasts of a pair of lovers. Hand in hand they have been seen walking the halls and stairs of the old structure at night. This is rather phenomenal considering neither the man nor woman has ever been reported being seen with a head. You could say in this incident, love was truly blind.

Some years ago near Monroe stood the Lemerick Plantation. It boasted of having been occupied by a fun loving, yet mischievous ghost. This ghost did not scare or terrify the

inhabitants, he did on the other hand keep their attention and let them know he was around. He would nightly send the stair spindles rolling down the stair case, one spindle at a time.

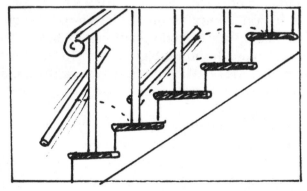

Not only are the plantation homes occupied by ghosts, the grounds, trees, bayous and rivers next to the plantations are also inhabited with these transparent, or sometimes cloud like creatures. In Pontchatoula, there is a haunted gum tree next to a plantation home that is haunted by a young woman. It was

reported that in her despair she hung herself from a limb of the tree. She, it could be said, still hangs around the old gum tree.

Near Marksville during the Civil War, Union and Confederate forces waged a fierce battle with many on both sides being killed. After the battle, a long trench was hurriedly dug and all

bodies buried in a common grave without benefit of religious services or segregation of the Union and Confederate soldiers. Those who were placed in this unblessed, unsegregated place over 100 years ago apparently cannot rest because of this mess up. They can still be seen marching at night when conditions are right, greys on one side of the trench and blues on the other.

In deep south Louisiana, close to Cut Off, land area that was once the location of the Mississippi River is said to be haunted. Many years ago the river, as it did so many times, changed its course, leaving a large steamboat loaded with valuable freight and an unhappy captain stranded high and dry. The captain was furious. He cursed the river, the steamboat, its passengers, and even himself. In a fit of anger he lost his cool. Without thinking, he wished they never got out of the place. As the old saying goes, "Ask and you shall receive." His wish was, to his dismay, granted. To this day, especially on foggy nights, although far from the river, you can still hear the sound of the paddle wheel, the boat's bell and the bellowing voice of the cantankerous captain cursing the river, the steamboat, his passengers, and above all himself, for making a wish that he should never have made.

Ghosts reported on Louisiana plantations for the most part, are like the citizens of the state. Almost all are of the friendly variety. Just as sugar or honey will attract more flies than salt, friendly ghosts no doubt attract more people than spooky, creepy or scary ghosts.

EMBELLISHMENT

DOUBLE CURVING STAIRWAYS (RECEPTION STAIRS)

These served a dual purpose. They were designed as symbols of welcome as though the owner had his or her arms outstretched. Ladies wore hoop skirts; therefore, they went up one side and the men went up the other. This eliminated the temptation of looking under a lady's skirt as she walked up the stairs.

WHISTLE WALK

The kitchens of plantation homes were never built as a part of the main building; they were always in a separate building.

This served two purposes, the first being safety in case of a fire. Furthermore, it eliminated additional heat in the living area.

Of course, food during the dinner hour had to be brought from the kitchen to the main dining room. The little boys that carried the food were required to whistle between the two points (one cannot chew and whistle at the same time) — therefore the term "whistle walk."

ONE OF A KIND

At the Walnut Grove Plantation, an ingenious method of delivering the food from the kitchen to the dining room table was used. It proved to be entertaining as well as an efficient means of getting the job done. The owner built a miniature railroad that delivered the food directly to the table quickly and always steaming hot.

IVORY BUTTON

Whenever walking into a plantation home you could tell instantly if the mortgage had been paid by looking at the main banister of the handrail on the ground level. If you saw an ivory button embedded in the head of the banister post, you could

rest assured the owner was proud of the fact the mortgage had been paid. The button was a subtle way of delivering this message without ever saying a word.

PUNKAH FAN

The finishing touch to a dining room whose table groaned at dinner time because of the vast variety of succulent, piping hot food is called the punkah fan.

Because of the heat and humidity in the summer months in

Louisiana, many of the finer plantation homes' dining rooms were furnished with the punkah fan. It was a wooden-framed flapping device fastened to the ceiling directly over the table. It was operated by slave boys who pulled a rope that slowly and rhythmically swung the flap back and forth the entire time diners were seated at the table.

SLAVE QUARTERS

It is a misconception that all slave quarters were built of wood because bricks were more costly than lumber. The reason bricks were not used stems from the fact slaves were extremely superstitious people. They believed bricks contained the evil spirits and would rather sleep out in the elements, no matter how severe the weather, rather than sleep in a brick-enclosed structure.

KING'S THRONE

We have all no doubt heard the term "the wee house behind the big house." That, of course, refers to the days before indoor plumbing. What did the wealthy plantation owner do to overcome this unpleasantness, you ask? They used what is called a "privy chamber." It was a chair with a hole in the seat

and a place beneath the chair for a chamber pot. For those desiring privacy, a "modesty curtain" was installed on the chair (curtain from floor to rod circling above the chair).

Because of Louisiana's European background, wealthy home owners used an armchair carved and decorated in Louis XIV motif. If you have ever heard the term "excuse me, I must hold court with Louis XIV," now you know what they meant. The other term, a little less delicate, but more commonly used, was "excuse me, I am going to sit on the throne."

NO CLOSETS

Armoire

When visiting old plantation homes, you will never see closets, and, in some cases, you'll see outside stairways leading to the second floor.

The reason: during the Spanish occupation of Louisiana, home owners were taxed on the number of rooms. Since closets and stairwells were classified as rooms, home owners, if they wished to beat the taxes, did not build closets or inside stairways.

PIGEONNIERS

A large number of plantations have pigeonniers, "pigeon houses." Many are made of wood, and some are made of brick. All are rather large and could accommodate a large flock of pigeons. Plantation owners throughout the state loved pigeons, especially homing and racing pigeons. They kept them not only as a hobby, but also for eating purposes. Young pigeons, called squabs, made a truly tasty dish when cooked properly. Trial and error proved that the ideal time to cook the squabs was when they were 28 days old.

OWNERS WENT APES OVER DRAPES

Plantation owners had lots of fun and spent tons of money building and furnishing their plantation homes. To prove they had an unending supply of money, all you had to do upon

entering a home was look on the floor of any room. What would you look for? Of all things, draperies. On the floor, you say? Yes, the beautiful and tall drapery-covered windows were ten, twelve and sometimes fourteen feet high, topped with an elaborate cornice. If the owner really had the moola, he would have the draperies made a foot or so longer than necessary, allowing a pool of draperies to spill onto the floor.

No doubt it was hoped the guests would drool upon seeing the pool of draperies on the floor. If they did, it was sure to bring a smile of satisfaction to the owner's face.

1990 LOUISIANA PLANTATIONS

Parish & District	No. of Plantations	Acres
St. Tammany	108	36,450
Tangiapahoa	108	21,219
Washington	218	78,059
D-3 TOTAL	434	35,728
Allen	634	93,035
Evangeline	80	17,746
Jeff Davis	4	661
D-2 TOTAL	718	111,442
Caldwell	180	14,346
Catahoula	104	23,101
Grant	281	20,640
LaSalle	658	45,339
Winn	781	49,439
D-3 TOTAL 2,004		152,865
Bienville	836	51,691
Bossier	262	10,439
Caddo	177	10,284
Claiborne	746	32,708
Webster	401	17,599
D-4 TOTAL	2,422	122,721
Jackson	725	44,200
Lincoln	647	21,425
Morehouse	178	7,690
Ouachita	184	12,007
Union	1,009	30,674
D-5 TOTAL	2,743	115,996

LOUISIANA PLANTATIONS

Parish & District	No. of Plantations	Acres
DeSoto	283	16,770
Natchitoches	575	40,785
Red River	216	6,870
Sabine	473	45,834
D-6 TOTAL	1,547	110,259
Beauregard	733	261,991
Calcasie	97	39,002
Vernon	676	236,248
D-7 TOTAL	1,506	537,241
Avovelles	6	213
Rapides	367	120,073
D-8 TOTAL	373	120,286
Concordia	5	593 E.
Carroll	4	685
Franklin	31	9,691
Madison	1	11,942
Richland	10	156
Tensas	3	2,098
W. Carrol	5	395
D-9 TOTAL	69	15,560
E. Baton Rouge	2	142 E.
Feliciana	62	4,238
Livingston	105	20,631
St. Helena	153	21,363
W. Feliciana	8	638
D-10 TOTAL	330	47,012
STATE TOTAL	12,146	1,469,110

CHAPTER 5

CIVIL WAR

INTRODUCTION
AMERICA'S INCREDIBLE CIVIL WAR — 1861 - 1865

From elegant living to the outhouse is how one man described Louisiana before and after the Civil War. Or as one lady put it, that unpleasant time in southern history.

During what was economically called the "Golden Era" in Louisiana in the 1850s and early 1860s, Louisiana ranked as the second wealthiest state per capita in the nation. The mighty Mississippi River carried freight from thirty-three states, and it all wound up in Louisiana ports. The ports of Louisiana were beehives of activity, not only during the daylight hours but at night as well.

The three principal crops up to this time in the history of North America were sugar, cotton and rice. Louisiana was blessed with fertile land capable of producing all three in astronomical quantities. Sugar alone was produced at 1,291 plantations, manned by 139,000 slaves. In 1859-60, 2,214,296 bales of cotton were handled at the port of New Orleans alone. The value of this one commodity was in excess of 185 million dollars. Rice plantations were producing record quantities per acre. Any plantation owner producing three successful crops in a row was virtually guaranteed becoming a millionaire. Because of the fertile soil, hard work and the blessing of good weather, crops in Louisiana before the Civil War were responsible for making more millionaires in the State of Louisiana than all the other states combined.

Louisiana found itself in a peculiar position on the eve of the Civil War. Louisiana had never espoused states' rights. Louisiana had strong economic ties to all of the United States. Because Louisiana agriculturally and economically depended on its connection with the rest of the Union, Louisiana had little, if any, cause to withdraw from the Union.

The fly in the ointment became apparent in 1859 when Abe Lincoln ran for the Presidency of the United States. Once Lincoln was in office, increasingly Louisiana citizens felt that the day of compromise had passed. They felt that even though Lincoln's views on slavery were moderate, his election was a clear signal that the time had come for the parting of the ways. The matter came to a head on January 26, 1861, when a vocal group of secessionists won control of a convention to consider Louisiana's future with the Union. By a large majority, an ordinance of secession was passed. For nine days, Louisiana became an independent republic. At this point, Louisiana joined the Confederacy. Once Louisiana became one of the Confederate States of America, forts on the Mississippi River were seized as were the Federal Mint and Custom House. Excitement was so thick in Louisiana you could cut it with a knife.

GEN. P. G. T. BEAUREGARD
GEN. WILLIAM TECUMSEH SHERMAN

Shortly before the Civil War began, Colonel William T. Sherman served in the capacity of Superintendent of LSU (he was the University's first superintendent). He left that position shortly before the war began because his sympathies were with the Union. On the other side of the ledger, General P.G.T.

Beauregard was serving as the Commandant of West Point. He left that prestigious post to join the Confederate forces. While in training at West Point, Beauregard's artillery instructor was Major Robert Anderson. This was to be another of the many ironies of the Civil War. The first battle between Confederate and Union forces took place at Fort Sumter. General Beauregard fired the first shot of the war. Anderson and Beauregard were at one time good friends; now they were mortal enemies, for Anderson was the Commandant of Fort Sumter. The official time and date of the first shot was 4:30 a.m., Friday, April 12, 1861. For the next thirty-six hours, four thousand shells were fired — but, not one mortal soul on either side was killed. Anderson's decision to surrender on the afternoon of April 13th was forced upon him, as Confederate shells set wooden buildings on fire in the central courtyard. Fire was spreading to Fort Sumter's main magazine, and, had it reached there, loss of human life would have been great.

Once the surrender was accomplished, Beauregard allowed Major Anderson and his gallant garrison of eighty-five soldiers to embark to the North aboard a Union ship. The first battle of the war was free of death on either side. It was not an omen of what turned out to be the most devastating war, in terms of loss of life, that this country has ever taken part in to this day.

NAMES AND FIRSTS

Never has there been a war that was called by so many names and introduced so many firsts in warfare as the United States of America versus the Confederate States of America.

NAMES CALLED	FIRST
War for Southern Independence	Repeating rifle
Second American Revolution	Machine gun
War for States' Rights	Flame thrower
Lincoln's War	Railroad artillery
Second War for Independence	Aerial reconnaissance
Brother's War	Fixed ammunition
War of Secession	Antiaircraft fire
War Between the States	Battle photography
Yankee Invasion	Aircraft carrier (balloons)
Confederate War	Naval torpedo
Lost Cause	Steel ship
War of North and South	Land - mine field
War of the Union	Successful submarine
War for Abolition	Military telegraph
War for Separation	Economic warfare (bogus money)
War Against Northern Aggression	Naval admiral Great
Rebellion	Naval smoke screen
War for Constitutional Liberty	Aerial psychological warfare
Southern Rebellion	Income tax - Cigarette tax
War of the Rebellion	U.S. Secret Service
War for Southern Rights	Anesthetic for wounded
	Medal of honor

FLAGS OF THE CONFEDERACY

The Southern states that seceded from the Union to form the Confederate States of America adopted their first flag on March 4, 1861. It was called the stars and bars. Because it looked so much like the federal flag, it caused confusion on the battlefield of Bull Run, requiring a second flag to be designed. This one was known as the "Battle Flag" and was ordered by the Confederate Congress. It has become the most recognized of the four Confederate flags. It was white with a union of red and blue saltier bordered in white and charged with 13 white stars. On March 4, 1865, the flag was altered and an upright red band was placed on the flying edge for visibility.

ST. FRANCISVILLE, LA.
MOST UNUSUAL INCIDENT

In the spring of 1863, St. Francisville was heavily involved in military activities of the Civil War. Grace Episcopal Church was right in the middle of the activities. The church's cornerstone had been laid by Leonidas Polk, known as "the fighting bishop from Louisiana," because of his dual role as a bishop as well as

a general of the Confederate Army. Because the church was located on top of a hill, the church tower made an excellent target for the federal gunboats patrolling the river.

During the shelling siege by the federal gunboats, the accurate cannon fire destroyed the belfry and inflicted severe damage to the beautiful church that was only three years old. A lull in the fighting became evident by the deafening silence. A small boat from the gunboat Albatross, with three officers, headed to shore, flying the flag of truce and carrying the dead body of Commander John E. Hart. They were met at the shore by Confederate Captain William W. Leake. He was informed that Commander Hart was a Mason, and on his death bed (he committed suicide) had requested a Masonic burial. Captain Leake, being a Mason himself, agreed to honor his fellow Mason's last wish. He selected local members of the Masonic order dressed in grey Confederate uniforms, along with an equal number of federal officers in their blues, and carried the remains of Captain Hart to the Grace Episcopal churchyard cemetery. The Masonic services were read by Confederate Captain Leake. Reverend S. D. Lewis, Rector of Grace Church, whose building was still smoldering from the cannon fire of

the Albatross, read the burial office. Upon completion of the services, burial was made in the Masonic plot and recorded by Reverend Lewis.

After the burial the three federal officers went back to the Albatross. The flag of truce was removed, and the military encounter resumed.

After the war, Commander Hart's final resting place was covered by a marble slab with the Masonic emblem etched into it.

This unusual incident, if nothing else, demonstrates the universal brotherhood of men within the bounds of Free Masonry.

BATTLE OF BATON ROUGE

At the outbreak of the Civil War in 1861, the people of Louisiana felt reasonably safe. Louisiana's location far beneath her sister states gave the people a false sense of security.

Therefore, little or nothing was done to prepare for an unexpected invasion in 1862. So certain were the military leaders that Baton Rouge and New Orleans would be safe from attack, military men from Louisiana and supplies seized in Louisiana from federal arsenals were sent to where the fighting was already taking place. Complacency led to shock in Baton Rouge, when they learned that Admiral Farragut had passed the only two forts on the Mississippi River below New Orleans and took New Orleans without any resistance.

All seven thousand Baton Rouge citizens, with very few military personnel to defend them, were in disbelief on May 7, 1862, when the Yankee gunboat Iroquois dropped anchor at their doorstep. All military personnel and most of the civilian population evacuated the city, turning it over to the Yankees without a single shot being fired. The Yankees, shortly after capturing Baton Rouge, left en masse and headed to Vicksburg to take part in the reduction of that city.

On May 29th, the Union Infantry, 2,600 strong, reentered

Baton Rouge led by General Thomas Williams, a West Point graduate. A tent city was set up and went as far as the eye could see. At Camp Moore, seventy miles east of Baton Rouge in Tangapahoa Parish, Governor John C. Breckenridge (former Vice President of the United States) learning of the infantry landing in Baton Rouge, made plans to attack and take Baton Rouge back. General Williams had 4,000 men in training, plus he was in telegraph communications with the captain of 165 foot iron-clad ram Arkansas that overwhelmed the Yankee fleet at Vicksburg.

The invasion to recapture Baton Rouge started by marching troops from Camp Moore. General Williams also requested the back up of the all important invincible Arkansas from Vicksburg. With this army and navy combination, the Confederates had every reason to feel confident of victory. The Yankees prepared entrenchments for their infantry, backed by their five naval ships in support. They were now ready. On August 5th, dawn was slow in coming. The fog that morning in Baton Rouge was very thick. At first light of dawn the attack began.

Some of the heaviest fighting, much of it hand to hand combat, took place in the Magnolia Street Cemetery. Many tombs and monuments were damaged as soldiers used them for protection during the fighting. Many are still chipped and gouged where mini balls struck them. After four hours of vigorous fighting the fog lifted. As soon as it did the federal gunboats began bombarding the Confederates.

Until this time everything was all going the Confederates way. The tide began to turn as soon as the fog lifted. Confederate losses started to rise. There were many ranking officers that were wounded and killed. This loss of leadership had a telling effect on the fighting. The five Union naval vessels continued a relentless bombardment of Confederate ranks, an indicator that the invincible ironclad Arkansas had not made the three hundred mile trip to Baton Rouge. It was later learned that the Arkansas' engine gave out four miles from Baton Rouge. It was of absolutely no assistance to the Confederate forces. Its commander blew the ship up rather than have it fall into the enemy's hands.

The battle was in its sixteenth hour of continuous fighting without time to eat or drink. Many areas were stacked several deep with blue and grey clad bodies. During the battle, the Yankee's General Williams was struck by a Rebel bullet and killed. Union ships continued to fire and slowly reduced the city to rubble. The Rebels had neither the physical nor material strength for a decisive push. With nothing to match the fire power of the naval guns the decision was made to bring the fighting to an end. The Confederate troops withdrew. The Yankee forces made no attempt to pursue them. The battle was considered a stalemate.

When the final count of casualties was made, four hundred and fifty-six Confederates and three hundred and eighty-three Union soldiers were killed. Many others were wounded or captured. In some cases the dead were buried in common shallow graves.

Like so many Civil War battles, the Battle of Baton Rouge

accomplished little. Although the Yankee forces fought and died to take the town, as soon as they were victorious, Union forces were evacuated from the city and went to New Orleans. As they moved out the Confederates moved right back into the town.

As though Baton Rouge was a revolving door, the Yankees re-occupied the city on December 17th. This time they left a lasting and devastating impression. On December 28th, a careless soldier cooking in the state capitol set it on fire. Despite efforts to save the building, it was only a blackened shell by morning.

SATURDAY, MARCH 15, 1863
FIRES OF JOY WAR

Each Christmas Eve on the river banks in lower Louisiana what the French called "Feux de Joie" ("Fires of Joy") have been lit for hundreds of years. This old custom was brought from Europe and has been celebrated in Louisiana since 1718, the year that New Orleans was founded. The purpose of the fires in Europe on Christmas Eve was twofold: First to light the way to the traditional midnight mass, and second, to express love to the neighbors and friends of those who were unable to attend mass and they would not see on Christmas.

During the Civil War at Port Hudson, located on the Mississippi River north of Baton Rouge, the fires of joy were used for military purposes. In the beginning of March 1863, the commander of the fort received word that Admiral Farragut's powerful fleet planned on passing the fort under the cover of darkness. The admiral surmised that what the gunners at the strategically located fort could not see, they could not hit.

A young confederate private who lived on the lower

Mississippi River told his commanding officer, Captain J. W. Youngblood, of the traditional Feux de Joi used at Christmas on the Mississippi River. Captain Youngblood suggested to Major General Franklin Gardner, who was in command of the Confederate Army of Mississippi and eastern Louisiana, that in order to stop the Admiral's Fleet from moving up River at night, he and a group of soldiers be assigned to go down river of the fort, and stack enormous piles of dead wood, logs, brush and trash along both sides of the river. He would then assign his men to stand watch around the clock. When the Admiral's Fleet started moving up the river, the bon fires would then be ignited to illuminate the target. The suggestion was implemented and proved to be highly successful. At exactly 11:22 p.m. on Saturday, March 15, 1863, the fleet started moving up river, fires on both sides were lit illuminating the ships and virtually made them sitting ducks. The entire area of the river occupied by the federal fleet was illuminated like the light of day. The guns of Port Hudson fired continuously. All pandemonium let loose. The devastation inflicted on the almost helpless federal fleet was enormous. The battle scene as described by the Colonel Isaiah Steedman of the First Alabama characterized it as "The grandest most sublime and terrible scene of my life." John Wilson of Lafayette County Mississippi recalled it as "The most beautiful sight I witnessed during the war. It looked like the heavens were on fire."

When the fighting was finally over, Admiral Farragut, after surveying the results learned he had suffered a crushing, humiliating defeat. The loss of lives on the federal ships was high. In contrast, only one confederate soldier from Tennessee was killed during the battle. Equally devastating were the number of ships that were sent to the bottom of the river. Every ship that was not sunk suffered severe damages. Admiral Farragut's Fleet was crippled for a long, long time.

As one confederate soldier put it, "The finger of God was with us." If credits were to be passed out, a lowly confederate private who made the suggestion of converting the "Fires Of

Joy" used at Christmas time to military use would without question receive the top award. Unfortunately his name has escaped the history books.

Note: Taking part in this great Confederate victory was an 18-year-old Lieutenant from Louisiana named Edward Douglas White, who years later became Chief Justice of the United States Supreme Court.

General Franklin Gardner, although a Northerner by birth and whose father was at one time Adjutant General of the Army of the North, was an idol to the Confederate troops he commanded. He was also the son-in-law of Louisiana Governor Alexandre Mouton.

RARE COINS — CONFEDERATE STATES OF AMERICA

Shortly after the Civil War began in 1861 the Confederate Army of New Orleans seized the United States Mint. The newly-formed government of the CSA made plans, without delay, to mint a half dollar coin. A die was prepared and four original half dollars were produced on a hand press at the now Confederate States of America Mint. One was given to the Secretary of the Confederacy, Memminger, who passed it on to President Jefferson Davis for his approval. Another was presented to Professor J. L. Redell of the University of Louisiana. Dr. E. Ames of New Orleans received a third, and the fourth was given to Chief Coroner B. F. Taylor. For unknown reasons mass production of this coin never came about. The coin was still unknown to collectors as late as 1879, fourteen years after the war ended. Over the past 127 years, these rare coins, scarce as hens' teeth, have passed no doubt through numerous hands and are at the top of the want lists of serious coin collectors around the world. One must be serious if they plan to obtain one of these rare coins, especially from a financial standpoint. The value of each of these coins today is estimated at $250,000.

SALT — WORTH ITS WEIGHT IN GOLD

Although it is not an item to which we give a second thought, salt is one of those items without which man cannot live. In tracing the history of man, you soon realize mankind has almost never inhabited areas where salt was not available. In parts of the world where cannibalism was practiced, it is believed by some historians that it — cannibalism — was due to necessity because of the absence of salt.

Before the Civil War, as well as after the war began, all salt used in the South came from England by way of the Port of New Orleans. When the mouth of the Mississippi River was blockaded after New Orleans fell, a serious problem was born. It is true that Judge Daniel D. Avery was producing salt using an elaborate salt evaporating process at Petite Anse Island (now Avery Island), ten miles southwest of New Iberia. Utilizing brine springs, the Judge was able to produce a small quantity of salt. When the salt supply from England was cut off, the salt produced by the Judge was considered more important than supplies of sugar, molasses, vegetables, pork, cotton, etc.

In May of 1862, an important discovery was made at Petite Anse Island by production manager John Avery, son of Judge Daniel Avery. While cleaning and deepening one of the salt springs, the slaves uncovered a huge rock salt bed just fifteen to twenty feet below ground level. Lucky for the Confederates, it was the first rock salt discovery in the continental United States. Some historians believe the war may have ended sooner were it not for the discovery. The tedious, time-consuming evaporation method to produce salt from the springs was immediately replaced by the quick, easy digging and loading directly into drums and then into wagons.

Major General Richard Taylor (son of U.S. President Zachary Taylor) Commander of Confederate forces in the district of western Louisiana, upon learning of the discovery through his intelligence personnel, assigned two companies of infantry and a section of artillery to safeguard the newly-found salt

mine against attack by the enemy. This alone showed the importance of the salt. Judge Avery immediately placed the mine at Taylor's disposal.

A small army of Negro workers was sent to the mine to work around the clock to extract the much-needed salt. Next on the agenda, a meat curing and packing facility was established in New Iberia. During the succeeding months, salt and salt beef were shipped by steamer to Port Hudson, Vicksburg and other Confederate ports east of the Mississippi.

In time, between four hundred and six hundred men were digging and loading salt day and night. At all times, anywhere from one hundred to five hundred wagons with teams of horses were on the grounds of the salt mine. They were from every section of the Confederacy. Each of the drivers entered the loading area with cash in his hand and a smile on his face. In the last year of the war, it is estimated Judge Avery received anywhere from two to three million dollars in cash for his much-needed salt. No doubt he, too, had a smile on his face, for his salt was as pure as driven snow and as valuable as gold.

MOST NOTORIOUS MILITARY OCCUPATION

Of all the Government officials and officers in the Union military services during the Civil War, none were close to being hated by Louisianians as much as Major General Benjamin Butler.

Butler arrived in Louisiana at the Port of New Orleans on May 1, 1862. This was the beginning of what was heralded as the most notorious military occupation of the War Between the States. Butler's reputation preceded him. As commander of the occupation forces, Louisiana leaders were fearful from the start that he would destroy the economy of the state. Their fears were well founded. Before Butler ended his seven-and-a-half-month reign, he earned the titles of "Beast Butler," because of his cruel treatment, and "Spoons Butler," because of all the silverware he confiscated during his occupation of New

Orleans. The 40-year-old ex-lawyer, with no previous military experience, but with good taste, took up residence at the plush St. Charles Hotel. He naturally had the presidential suite. His equally pompous brother, Andrew Jackson Butler, served as his aide — and we think nepotism is new! General Butler was a fat, ungainly man with a high-pitched voice, and what some labeled, "cocked eyes." These features alone made it easy to poke fun at him. Butler wasn't in town long before he began, as the old saying goes, creating waves. He started off by requiring his enemies to take the oath of allegiance to the United States. Those who refused had their property confiscated and were subject to deportation. It is said that the majority of the silverware confiscated never made it to the federal warehouses. Butler knew of the pride of the people of

the area, reference their beloved statue of Andrew Jackson. For pure unadulterated spite, he had the inscription "The Union Must And Shall Be Preserved" deeply engraved into the base of the statue. He knew this would infuriate the citizens. He was one hundred percent correct. They would have preferred having their bodies disfigured than the defacing of the monument.

Soon after New Orleans fell, but before the city had formally surrendered, Butler made an example of 42-year-old William

B. Munford, who, being sympathetic to the Confederacy, tore down the American flag flying from the flagpole on top of the mint on Esplanade Avenue. Gallows were built in front of the mint, and Munford was hung before a large crowd that was

required to witness one of Butler's evil deeds. To say the least, they were shocked and angry.

Because New Orleans' Mayor John T. Monroe refused to take down the Confederate flag that was flying over city hall, Butler sentenced him and his adviser Pierre Soulé to federal prison. When three Episcopalian ministers refused to pray for the President of the United States, he exiled them. These were only some of the miseries inflicted by the "Beast." By committing all of these dastardly deeds on the people of New Orleans, Butler found himself surrounded by hostility, hatred and harassment in every imaginable form. In a parade, he was characterized by an unknown masker who had the body of a big, fat hyena, with a sword on his belt, a skull in one hand and carrying a large silver spoon in the other. A sign signifying who this character was, was not needed. Butler, upon seeing it, became furious but said nothing. When the "Beast" walked the streets, people mimicked his high-pitched voice. Others looked him straight in the eyes and crossed theirs. Fat, bald men when passing him on the street stuck out their bellies and rubbed their hands across their bald heads. He said nothing; he just bit his tongue to control his temper. Citizens used every occasion possible to ridicule Butler as well as his officers. Not only did men take part in this form of retaliation, women of the city, including those of the upper class, directed their taunts towards the unwelcome tyrant. Butler's patience reached the boiling point. He could take no more. This was the straw that broke the camel's back. His knee-jerk reaction was to be written and talked about all the way to the most northern Union state and across the ocean. On May 15, 1862, General Butler issued the most controversial ordinance of the war.

General Order #28 did stop the insults, but the results of the order, suggesting treating the ladies of New Orleans as prostitutes, served as fuel to flame the determination of all southern forces. Confederate President Jefferson Davis sent a letter of denunciation to Butler. Letters from southern editors, as well as from the northern press, were sent to "The Beast." Confederate generals seized the opportunity to rally their troops by reading General Order #28 to their men, not once, but whenever they felt it would serve their purpose. The story of General Ordinance #28 even reached the British Parliament, where Lord Palmerston said, "An Englishman must blush to

```
General Order           HEADQUARTERS DEPARTMENT OF THE GULF

No. 28.                     New-Orleans, May 15, 1862.


    As the officers and soldiers of the United States have been

subject to repeated insults from the women (calling themselves

ladies) of New Orleans, in return for the most scrupulous non-

interference and courtesy on our part, it is ordered that hereafter

when any female shall, by word, gesture, or movement, insult or

show contempt for any officer or soldier of the United States, she

shall be regarded and held liable to be treated as a woman of the

town plying her avocation.


    By command of                    MAJOR-GENERAL BUTLER

GEO. C. STRONG, A.A. Gen., Chief of Staff.
```

think such an act had been committed by a man belonging to the Anglo-Saxon race."

Although General Butler was born in poverty, it was reputed that he and his associates — especially his brother — made fortunes for themselves while in Louisiana by illegal and extralegal practices. If their wealth lasted as long as Butler's rotten reputation, no doubt their heirs are still well heeled.

PIONEER — FIRST SUBMARINE BUILT IN THE CONFEDERACY

On March 29, 1862, an application for the first submarine to be built by the Confederate Navy was filed. Pioneer, as she was named, was scheduled to be built in Louisiana at an Algiers shipyard. Plans indicated the ship would weigh four tons, be 34 feet in length, four feet in breadth and four feet deep. Her design was to have conical ends and once constructed was to be painted black. Records also stipulated a magazine of explosives would be carried. The crew would be made up of two or more. The commanding officer was located well forward within easy reach of the diving lever, rudder control, depth gauge and air cock. The course was laid on the surface and held by a set screw on the rudder. A magnetic compass lighted by a candle was used to detect variations from the desired direction. Fresh air was brought into the sub by way of an air shaft (it looked like a present day submarine periscope). A very small portion of the submarine was above the water line, and she only dived when a ship was within close range. Propulsion

was created when crew members operated a crank shaft that turned the propeller.

When construction was completed, a successful trial run, including blowing up a barge was achieved. Unfortunately the Pioneer never saw action. When New Orleans fell it is believed the Pioneer was purposely sunk in Lake Pontchartrain on April 27, 1862 to prevent capture by Admiral Farragut. Another version states that she went down on a trial run drowning all crew members.

The way the submarine operated is as follows: when the commanding officer saw the target, he would dive under the enemy towing a floating torpedo. Once the submarine passed the enemy ship and the torpedo came in contact with the hull, it would then and only then (hopefully) explode.

Sixteen years after the war, the Pioneer was accidentally found by some young boys who were swimming in Lake Pontchartrain. The wreck was brought to the surface and placed on shore until 1907. In that year the Pioneer was brought to Camp Nicholls, Home for Confederate Soldiers. It was proudly displayed on a block of concrete. Later the sub was moved to the ground floor, outside display area, of the Presbytere where it has remained until today.

The sub on display at the Presbytere is not 34 feet in length as indicated in the drawings. It is believed by some, that when retrieved and put on shore, numerous parts were missing. Other parts were removed by vandals during the land stay. This would, of course, lead to the smaller version that is on display at the Presbytere. Others, on the other hand, feel that the sub at the Presbytere is not the Pioneer, but another ship.

H. L. HUNLEY — FIRST SUBMARINE IN HISTORY TO SINK A SHIP

Although the builders of the submarine Pioneer did not attain their goal of sinking an enemy ship, their spirits were not dampened. Headed by a wealthy Louisianian H. L. Hunley, the marine engineering team of vision was made up of Baxter Watson, James R. McClintoch and Robert R. Barrow. When New Orleans fell into enemy hands, they moved their submarine operation to Mobile, Alabama (just a half hour drive from today's nuclear sub pen at Pascagoula, Mississippi) and set up operation at Parks and Lyons Machine Shop. It was there they met a seasoned British machinist, William A. Alexander, who joined the group. McClintoch and Watson worked nonstop and came up with a new design, Hunley furnished the money, and Alexander handled the fabrication of a new vessel. Once completed, the maiden trial was anxiously awaited by all. The results brought good and bad news. The bad news was the ship sank; the good news was that no lives

OCT. 15 1863

were lost. A different approach with a new design was worked on. When completed, the sub was given the name H. L. Hunley, for its financier. This sub was made by cutting a 25 foot long boiler in half lengthwise. After this was completed, crude ballast tanks were fabricated just under the skin. There was an air box fitted to a shaft so that fresh air could be admitted at will, provided the ship was quite near the surface. Propulsion was generated by an eight-man crew turning a crank fabricated from an iron shaft. To protect the propeller, an iron shield was attached to the end of the shaft. A torpedo, towed at the end of a 200 foot rope was the device designed to blow up enemy ships.

On Hunley's first trial run, she achieved her mission, sinking a flat boat. Elation was followed by deafening silence. As the ship returned to port, she ran into rough water in Mobile Bay and sank. In this accident, it is not known how many or if all members of the crew were lost. The sub was again raised and refurbished. When work was completed, the little ship was then sent to Charleston, S.C. by rail in the hopes of helping General Beauregard loosen the blockade of that city.

Upon arrival, a new crew was taken on, headed by Lieutenant John Payne. The crew was trained, and the ship was believed ready for combat. After Captain Payne lit a candle, the crew made their way to their cranking stations. Once everyone was in place, Payne let water into the tanks until the sub lay three inches under water. The cocks were then closed, and the ship was now ready to shove off. Before they left the dock, disaster again struck when the wake of a passing steamer washed over

Water line when ballested to sink
water line light

the deck, swamping the ship and sinking her. Payne was the only member of the crew to escape. Like a yo-yo, the ship was raised again. Lieutenant Payne was no doubt a super salesman, for he took on yet another crew. Another trial run and another crew was lost. Lieutenant Payne must have had nine lives, because this time he and only two others made it to safety. General Beauregard, at this point, lost all faith in the ship's seaworthiness. It took H. L. Hunley and his persuasive ability many hours of arguing with Beauregard to get an okay for another trial run to be headed by Hunley himself. It looked as if things were ready to turn around for the seemingly snake-bitten vessel. This trial run proved to be a complete success. Before they could savor their achievements, a major disaster struck on October 15, 1863. Not only did the sub sink drowning the entire crew; also a victim was financier and promoter H. L. Hunley.

Beauregard was at his wits' end. He insisted there would be no more trials and no more loss of life until the sub was raised and examined thoroughly. After this was done, it was decided that in the interest of safety the ship should carry torpedoes on a spar at the bow rather than tow the explosives with a rope. Although this was a minor change it proved to be a great improvement. Another volunteer crew was found, in spite of being told of all the past failures and drownings. This crew went through weeks of intensive training. The sub, during this training period, was tested to see how long she could stay submerged. The longest time recorded was two hours and thirty-five minutes.

The H. L. Hunley was once again believed ready for its long-awaited mission of destruction. The Federal fleet was aware that their enemy had a strange new craft that might be capable of a sneak attack. Admiral John Dahlgren advised all ship captains to be diligent in their watch. The evening of February 17, 1864, was a bright, clear, moonlit night, and the waters were calm. It was clear enough for lookouts standing on the gangway, forecastle and quarterdeck of the Housatonic to see all the other ships in the fleet. Just before 9:00 p.m., Acting Master J. K. Crosby was on the quarterdeck when he saw an object he believed to be a porpoise. The ship's quartermaster also saw it through his field glasses; he thought it was a school of fish. As the object got closer, Crosby could stand the suspense no longer and sounded the alarm calling all hands to quarters. As the crew scurried to their positions, Crosby ordered the anchor lifted. Officers and men poured onto the deck. The unknown object got closer and closer. Men on deck, including the captain who made his way to the bridge, saw a trailing phosphorescent light coming from the slow-moving object. Cannon fire was ordered by the captain, but to no avail. The mysterious object was so close to the Housatonic that its guns' muzzles could not be lowered far enough to hit the object. Several men shot rifles and muskets without obvious effect. In desperation, the Captain took aim and fired at the sub with a shotgun. No longer at anchor, the Housatonic was drifting with the current toward the oncoming craft. The Captain ordered the engines at full speed hoping to generate enough power to move out of the way of the approaching object. Before the turn could be maneuvered, the ship and the sub, each with its own momentum, rammed each other. This was

followed by a thunderous explosion. Timber and other parts of the Housatonic were blown into the air along with the Captain. Water began rushing into the hull as heavy black smoke belched from the ship's stack. The Captain miraculously landed in the bay unhurt. Just four minutes after the explosion, the 207-foot long armed screw-steamer sank like a stone in twenty-eight feet of water. When all hands on the Housatonic were picked up by the other ships in the area, only five Union sailors had been lost. The H. L. Hunley and its entire crew were also missing. The force of the impact fused the two ships. When the Housatonic went down, it dragged the H. L. Hunley, later nicknamed "The Coffin," with her.

The Housatonic was the first ship in history to be sunk by a submarine. The H. L. Hunley was the first successful submarine used for military purposes and, until World War I, the only American sub to sink an enemy ship.

After the war, Federal divers found the remains of the Housatonic. Divers also reported seeing the submarine nearby. One of the divers claimed that he even touched her propeller. To clear the channel of Charleston harbor the Housatonic was blown up.

In spite of the location being known, modern day divers with highly sophisticated equipment have not been able to locate the history-making submarine.

The H. L. Hunley story is a tribute to man's determination and to what lengths he will go to accomplish what had never been done before. The first successful military submarine stayed submerged a maximum of two hours and thirty-five minutes and had a range of a couple of miles (possibly with the number of sinkings, it traveled in its lifetime as much vertically as it did horizontally). Comparing the hand-cranked Hunley to today's atomic subs that can stay submerged for months at a time and go halfway around the world, you can say unequivocally that man has come a long way in underwater travel.

In achieving its goal of sinking an enemy ship, it is ironic that the lives of five or possibly six eight-man crews, plus the designer, builder and the man who financed the sub were all lost in the undertaking.

Note: The sub bore no Confederate device. She was owned by private parties and built for the profitable business of sinking enemy vessels as prizes. Builders had a title of marque for underwater privateering from a New Orleans collector of customs dated 1862.

DONALDSONVILLE SHELLING — EVERLASTING UNPLEASANT MEMORIES AND MISERIES

Donaldsonville, located on the west bank of the Mississippi River below Baton Rouge, was the state capital of Louisiana in 1830-31. Shortly after the Civil War started, New Orleans and Baton Rouge both fell into Yankee hands.

In 1862, all Federal ships going from New Orleans to Baton Rouge were being harassed as they passed Donaldsonville by sniper fire from a group of partisan Texas Rangers. It didn't matter if they were military vessels or, in some cases, steamboats carrying women and children. Captain James A. McWaters of the Texas Rangers did not realize the disastrous consequences that he was about to impose on the city of Donaldsonville by his actions. The mayor of Donaldsonville pleaded with McWaters to discontinue his antics, for the mayor had been warned by the Federals that, if these actions were not discontinued, the town would be shelled and he would inflict everlasting unpleasant memories on the town.

He responded by advising the mayor he would first have to discuss it with Louisiana's Governor Moore. On July 31st, the governor called a conference in Thiboudux. Governor Moore apparently overruled the mayor's pleas for McWaters's return to Donaldsonville and continued to fire on Union vessels.

Admiral Farragut, being a man of his word, sent a number of gunboats to Donaldsonville and carried out his threat. The

shelling was continuous for seven hours, inflicting much damage. When the shelling stopped, he carried out the second part of his threat — to inflict everlasting unpleasant memories and miseries. He sent a detachment ashore with torches. They proceeded to burn the business section of town, including the building that once served as the state's capitol. Some of the plantations along the river were also levelled. Upon leaving, the torch bearers left the following message from Admiral Farragut for the mayor, "Every time my boats are fired upon I will burn another portion of your town."

Apparently knowing Admiral Farragut to be a man of his word, sniper fire after this incident was discontinued by the Confederate forces.

Chances are, because of these everlasting unpleasant memories and miseries, the people of Donalsonville are not friendly to Texans in general. The general feeling was, "May the Bird of Paradise fly up their noses with claws extended."

DAMMED AND GLAD OF IT

During the Civil War, a fleet of federal gunboats was trapped by low water in the Red River. The commander of the fleet saw gloom and doom all over the situation. His gunboats stuck to the bottom, unable to maneuver, made his fleet sitting ducks. A staff meeting was called to alert everyone of the seriousness of the calamity. One of the officers, an ingenious civil engineer as a civilian, advised the captain that the seemingly hopeless situation was not as bad as it seemed. He suggested the problem could be solved with a little engineering ingenuity. The captain, knowing of the officer's expertise, turned the dilemma over to him. The officer had the brains and the plan; what he needed now was brawn. All available hands were immediately mustered. Under his direction, they proceeded to build a temporary dam made of mud and bolstered with heavy timbers. This resulted in retaining enough water to float the ships down to just above the dam. Once this was achieved, the dam was blown up. The rushing water literally flushed the ships downstream to deeper water and safety.

This, of course, proved that the old saying, "Where there is a will, there is a way," has meaning.

BATTLE OF LIBERTY PLACE

After the Civil War ended, the fighting in Louisiana was not really over; there was one main battle after the South surrendered. Carpetbag rule (or misrule as most Louisianian's claimed) was the beginning of the darkest days in Louisiana's political history. During these turbulent times, taxes increased 500%, and services were nil. Prewar legislative sessions cost less than $100,000.00 — carpetbag legislative sessions exceeded one million dollars. The state debt before the war was six million. In short order, the state debt rose 50 million dollars. Because of the blatant misuse of state funds, Louisiana was bankrupt and could not even pay the interest on its debt. Governor Henry Clay Warmoth, a carpetbagger from Illinois, with a salary of only $8,000 a year, amassed a fortune at a phenomenal rate. His indiscretions were so blatant, he was impeached. President Ulysses S. Grant replaced him with a temporary governor named P.B.S. Pinchback. Pinchback became the first black man in the history of the United states to serve as governor of any state.In the next gubernatorial election, John McEnery, a liberal Louisiana Democrat, ran against a Vermont carpetbagger named William Pitt Kellogg. Even though McEnery received seven thousand more votes

than Kellogg, Kellogg was declared "Elected" by the radical returning board. Although Louisiana citizens thought things had gotten as bad as they could, they were in for the shock of their lives as conditions deteriorated even further. As the New York Tribune printed a few years later, Louisiana's legislature was filled with thieves, adventurers, barbers, boot blacks, bartenders and confidence men. Offices were sold to the highest bidders. Business was brought to the point that nothing could be bought or sold, except votes.

In 1874, in the small town of Coushatta in north Louisiana, the people rioted en masse when they learned arms of all private citizens in Louisiana were to be confiscated. Under this order, Louisiana would be the only state where a man could not walk the streets carrying a gun. Next, Governor Kellogg issued an order to intercept and seize the Steamboat Mississippi as she headed to New Orleans carrying guns and ammunition. This action precipitated the gathering on September 14th of the members of the White League of Louisiana. They met in New Orleans on the neutral ground on Canal and St. Charles Streets by the statue of Henry Clay. Kellogg's abdication was asked for and unanswered, leading to the crowd's determination to drive out the usurper. At approximately 2:30 p.m., the White League and Kellogg's metropolitan police began what was labeled in the newspaper, "The Battle of Liberty Place". The battle involved thousands of men on each side. Each side had rifles, machine guns and cannons. When Kellogg's metropolitan police were finally driven out, losses to the White League were 16 killed, 45 wounded. The metropolitan police — 11 killed, 60 wounded. Although the White League won the battle, President Ulysses S. Grant sent in 5,000 additional Federal troops to restore order and return the government to Kellogg.

LIBERTY PLACE MONUMENT

   On November 15, 1882, an ordinance was passed ded-
icating the neutral ground on Canal Street between Wells and
Delta Streets — location where fighting was the heaviest — for
the erection of a monument. The area would be known as
Liberty Place.

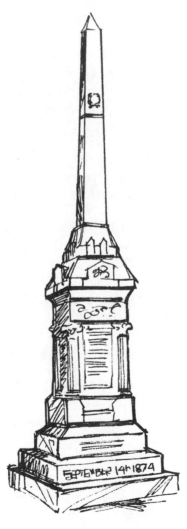

The cornerstone for the monument was laid on September 14, 1899. Chiseled into the monument are the names of the 16 men from Louisiana who were killed in the battle. The monument has the following inscription:

"IN HONOR OF THOSE WHO FELL IN DEFENSE OF CIVIL LIBERTY AND HOME RULE IN THAT HEROIC AND SUCCESSFUL STRUGGLE OF THE 14TH OF SEPTEMBER, 1874."

LITTLE KNOWN FACTS

A virtually unknown young Louisiana private namd Edward Douglas White took part in the battle. In later years, he became Chief Justice of the United States Supreme Court.

More Americans were killed at the Battle of Liberty place than at the Battle of New Orleans.

BITS AND PIECES

WHY CALLED BY SOME THE BOYS' WAR

Authorities differ, and statistics vary as they often do reference the Civil War, but according to the <u>Photographic History of the Civil War</u>:

FEDERAL SOLDIERS

More than 2,000,000 Federal soldiers were twenty-one or under (of a total of some 2,700,000).

More than 1,000,000 were eighteen or under.

About 800,000 were seventeen or under.

About 200,000 were sixteen or under.

About 100,000 were fifteen or under.

Three hundred were thirteen or under — most of these fifers or drummers, but regularly enrolled, and sometimes fighters.

Twenty-five were ten or under.

A study of a million Federal enlistments turned up only 16,000 as old as forty-four, and only 46,000 of twenty-five or more.

Commander-in-Chief Winfield Scott was 75 years old when the war began. He was the oldest Federal officer.

CONFEDERATE SOLDIERS

Records of the CSA were not as organized as the Federal's. It is known that the average age was much higher. The oldest Confederate noncommissioned soldier to serve was seventy-three years old.

700,000 DIED!!!

At least 618,000 Americans died in the Civil War, and some experts say the toll reached 700,000. At any rate, these casualties exceed the nation's loss in all its other wars, from the Revolution through Viet Nam.

The union armies had from 2,500,000 to 2,750,000 men. Their losses, by the best estimate:

Battle deaths:	110,070
Disease, etc.:	250,152
Total:	360,222

The Confederate strength, known less accurately because of missing records, was from 750,000 to 1,250,000. Its estimated losses:

Battle deaths:	94,000
Disease, etc.:	164,000
Total:	258,000

GETTYSBURG — BATTLE OF BLOOD

There were many fierce battles fought during the Civil War. The battle of Gettysburg was the bloodiest. It recorded 40% more dead, wounded and missing than any other Civil War battle.

Union		Confederate
3,155	dead	3,903
14,529	wounded	18,735
5,365	missing	5,425
23,049	total	28,063

Grand Total: 51,112. Duration, three days.

3,000 PLUS ADDITIONAL DEATHS

At this famous battle over 3,000 horses were also killed.

STATUES

Although there has never been a survey or a listing of all Civil War statues in Louisiana, it would be safe to bet the Civil War has more then any other. You could go even further and say there are more than any other two or even three wars combined. With an estimated 700,000 killed it is not that hard to comprehend why there are so many statuary remembrances.

The following are three examples:

COLONEL CHARLES DIDIER DREUX

First Confederate officer from Louisiana killed in the War Between the States. He was only 28-years-old when mortally wounded July 15, 1861, near Newport News, Virginia. His last words as inscribed on his monument were "Boys Steady." Although his monument was moved to its present location on Canal Street in New Orleans from the Rose Hill Cemetery when the burial ground was abandoned, he remained steadfast in his belief in the Confederate States of America and gave his life for that belief.

JEFFERSON DAVIS
ONLY AMERICAN PRESIDENT BURIED IN LOUISIANA

Jefferson Davis was also the only President of the Confederate States of America. He died in Louisiana, on December 6, 1889, and was entombed temporarily in the tumulus of the Army of Northern Virginia in Metairie Cemetery. This was a singularly appropriate gesture since it was the same Army of North Virginia that fought and bled to protect Richmond, the Capital of the Confederacy. President Davis's remains were later removed from Louisiana to Hollywood Cemetery in Richmond.

GENERAL ALBERT PIKE

The wordy inscription on his statue memorializes Pike as a soldier, philosopher and scholar. Pike's was a stormy career. He was believed by some to be the most controversial figure in America during the 19th century. He was accused of helping

Nathan Bedford Forrest set up the Ku Klux Klan, as well as participating in devil worship.

On the other side of the ledger, he was considered a brilliant attorney, a poet, gourmand, orator and friend of the American Indian.

Pike no doubt had a great deal of ability for he was not only a Confederate General, he was also elevated to the lofty position of 33rd degree Mason.

He is fondly remembered by most as a talented man whose problems stemmed from the troubled times he lived in.

THANKS, BUT NO THANKS.
IT COULD LEAD TO WASTE.

Even though the federal ordinance officer was offered Spencer repeating breech-loading rifles in 1860, he turned them down. The theory for his refusal — soldiers would fire too fast and waste ammunition. Repeating rifles did finally get into the fighting, but not until the very end of the war. Had repeating rifles been used from the start of the war who knows what the death toll would have been.

It was reported that firing on both sides was so inaccurate that it was estimated it took a man's weight in lead to kill a single enemy in battle.

MUSIC, MUSIC, MUSIC

The Union Army had a passion for military music. When the war began, there were 618 Union military bands. When this was learned by the congress, protests were heard throughout the Union. They were not sweet and melodious sounds, but heated choruses of protest. Research revealed that the War Department was spending 4 million dollars a year on bands, plus the unbelievable fact that there was one musician for every 41 soldiers. With these startling statistics uncovered, regimental bands became a thing of the past. From then on only brigades had official bands, each made up of a maximum of 16 musicians.

SUPREME COURT JUDGES

Of the future members of the United States Supreme Court who were of fighting age during the war, seven were in uniform. Four fought for the Union: Oliver Wendell Holmes, John M. Harlan, William B. Woods, and Stanley Matthews. Three fought for the Confederacy: Edward D. White, Horace H. Lurton and Lucius Q. C. Lamar.

THE BIG BANG

The "biggest manmade explosion in history" was planned for the demise of the ship Louisiana, set adrift with 215 tons of fused powder in an effort to destroy Fort Fisher, near Wilmington, North Carolina. The scheme, conceived by General Benjamin Butler, failed because of poor fuses, and the "A-bomb Of The Civil War" became a dud.

TWO CHOICES

General Robert E. Lee of Virginia was offered the position of military commander of both the North and the South forces. He accepted the position with the Confederate States of America simply because he had more relatives in the South than in the North.

Robert E Lee

WHAT A WAY TO BE REMEMBERED!!!

GEN. HOOKER

Union General Hooker will long be remembered, even though he would rather not have the notoriety in this particular instance. When General Hooker took command of the Army of the Potomac, his realistic policy towards recreation for his troops changed Washington overnight. Under Hooker's command, all red-light districts were allowed to flourish. Because of this action, the term "hooker" is associated with "Ladies of the Evening." Hooker's permissive behavior, if left unchecked, could have caused the downfall of the Union for the following reason: In 1861 the Union Army Medical Department in Washington reported that one out of every 12 soldiers had venereal disease.

LOUISIANA DID ITS PART

In 1861 Louisiana had 23,577 men in uniform. This was the largest number of men serving the Confederacy from any southern state based on population.

It was second only to Virginia in total numbers.

MULTINATIONAL REGIMENTS

Of all the regiments on both sides, the 1st Louisiana was probably the champion mixed regiment, for it sported men of thirty-seven nationalities. The Deep South furnished so many men of French nativity and descent that the Confederate army had two "official languages." In testimony to this fusion, General Beauregard invented the expression, "sacredamn."

LOUISIANA ZOUAVE REGIMENTS

Of the three Louisiana Zouave (a French infantry unit originally composed of Algerians wearing a brilliant uniform and conducting quick spirited drills) regiments, the most famous was named "Louisiana Tigers." They were commanded by capable and highly respected Crimean War veteran, Rob Wheat. It was said he was as tough on his troops as he was on the enemy. He was fair, but firm. Those who were insubordinate he simply had shot. Wheat honed the regiment to become a mean, fierce, fighting machine highly respected by the enemy. The regiment distinguished itself throughout the war, but their fierce, determined, fighting in the Valley of Shenandoah was what elevated them to the top echelon of Civil War fighting units. Just as the Tiger is classified "King of the Jungle," the Louisiana Tigers were superior on the battlefield.

In 1896, the LSU football team used for the first time the Tiger as their mascot in honor of the fierce Zouave Louisiana Tiger regiment. Like the Civil War Louisiana Tigers, they were fierce fighters honed to perfection by their football coach A. W. Jeardeau. He too was a disciplinarian. According to all records searched, thankfully no member of the team was ever shot for insubordination.

It is only fitting that in 1896, the very first year the LSU football team used the Tiger as its mascot they went undefeated. It was truly a great tribute to those they paid homage to.

CHAPTER 6

WEATHER

INTRODUCTION

SEMITROPICAL

HURRICANES

TORNADOES

LIGHTNIGNG

FLOODS

RAIN, SNOW AND ICE

MISCELLANEOUS

INTRODUCTION

Louisiana, when it comes to the weather, is built like some people, upside down. Their noses run and their feet smell.

The most predictable thing about the weather in Louisiana is its unpredictability. One would believe to have a sure bet if he wagered the hottest weather recorded in the state took place in the southern part and the heaviest snowfall was recorded in the northern section. With that twin bet he would be wrong in both instances. Louisiana's highest temperature, 114 degrees Fahrenheit, was recorded on August 10, 1936, in Plain Dealing. That's about as far north as one can go without leaving the state. On the other hand, the heaviest snowfall, 22" in a 24-hour period, was recorded on February 14, 1895, in, of all places, Lake Charles. That is very close to being the most southern part of the state.

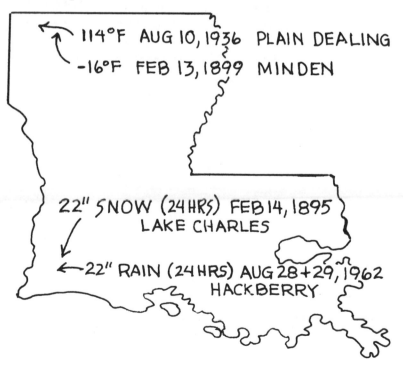

114°F AUG 10, 1936 PLAIN DEALING
-16°F FEB 13, 1899 MINDEN

22" SNOW (24HRS) FEB 14, 1895
LAKE CHARLES

22" RAIN (24HRS) AUG 28+29, 1962
HACKBERRY

Those two areas of the state also hold two other extreme weather records. Hackberry, located just a few miles south of Lake Charles, in a 24-hour period on August 28 and 29, 1962, recorded 22 inches of rain. The coldest temperature ever recorded, minus 16 degrees Fahrenheit, was on February 13, 1899, in Minden, just a few miles from where the record high was recorded.

As the old saying goes, "If you don't like the weather in Louisiana, just wait a few hours and it is sure to change."

LOUISIANA'S METEOROLOGICAL RECORDS

Monthly Average Temperatures In This Century (F.)

January	52.4	July	82.1
February	54.7	August	81.7
March	61.4	September	78.5
April	68.7	October	69.2
May	74.9	November	60.0
June	80.3	December	54.6

SOUTH LOUISIANA — SEMITROPICAL

Because of its geographic location, the southern part of the state of Louisiana is considered semitropical. New Orleans, the largest city in the state, located in the deep south, has as its oldest section, the historic French Quarter.

When visiting the French Quarter, you immediately notice the narrowness of the streets; also obvious is the fact that every building in each square of ground butts up against its neighbor. Once you enter the buildings you see that each patio is surrounded by high brick walls. The narrow streets, buildings butting against each other and walled-in patios are not by chance, they are by design and for a very good reason. Those who live in south Louisiana know that the summers are usually very hot and humid. Because of the design of the New Orleans French Quarter, the hot summer sun has to be directly overhead in to warm things up. Due to this unique design, the French Quarter patios, streets and buildings are in the shade most of the time.

Being semitropical, the humidity is as stated high and quite noticeable to visitors. It seems a little strange that in this

writer's travels to many areas with the same climatic conditions as south Louisiana, I have never heard anyone say anything about the unbearable humidity. It is only in south Louisiana I have heard unkind remarks concerning the humidity. Louisianians have, because of the frequency of this kind of statement, learned to respond in a positive way. They tell the visitors, both women and men in Louisiana love the high humidity. The females enjoy the humidity for it helps soften their skin and helps them to manage their hair. As one man put it, reference why men like it, he responded that he got out of an elevator in a high rise building in south Louisiana in August and the humidity was so high, six good-looking females stuck to him. Yes, this only proves that with a positive attitude every stumbling block can be turned over and made into a stepping stone.

While speaking of south Louisiana, a strange phenomenon occurred in New Orleans at the turn of the century. It occurred because of the city being almost entirely below sea level, and receiving an average annual rainfall of approximately sixty inches. Because of these conditions, New Orleans is probably the only place in the world where artificial changes in its natural physical conditions have been extensive enough to change the temperature of the overlying atmosphere.

This deduction was made by Dr. I.M. Cline, internationally noted meteorologist who served as the chief of the U.S. Weather Bureau in Louisiana for over 30 years. His statistical data covered 15 years before and after the city's subsurface drainage system was installed in 1900. Cline's statistics pointed out that from 1885 to 1899 New Orleans had never reported 100 degrees, and from 1900 to 1914 temperatures of 100 degrees and over were recorded in approximately 50% of those years. From 1885 to 1899, 95 degrees or higher were recorded only 35 days, and from 1900 to 1914, 74 days of 95 degrees or higher were recorded. It was also noted the average daily temperatures were higher in the latter period.

The cause of this phenomenon was the installation of subsurface drainage that drastically reduced the water tables in the city. Water in the drainage canals was lowered in 1900 by eight to ten feet. Dry land is heated much more rapidly by solar radiation than by water. Equal quantities of heat acting on equal areas of land and water increase the temperature of land nearly twice as fast as they do the temperature of water.

One sure proof that south Louisiana is semitropical lies in the fact that last year winter was very short. It was on a Wednesday, in the late afternoon!

HURRICANES
THE GREATEST STORMS ON EARTH

Good news and bad news both come with the first day of September. The good news is the fact that hurricane season, June 1 — November 30, is half over. The bad news is, of the six hurricane months, September is by far the most active.

September hurricanes have not been kind to Louisiana. History tells us the first storm recorded in the Gulf of Mexico was on September 19, 1599. It was recorded in a Spanish Marine Journal and was referred to as a "tempest" (a violent wind storm). September 11, 1722, is recorded in history as being the date of the first storm that hit Louisiana. It was undoubtedly a severe storm, for records tell us it knocked down every building in the city of New Orleans including the church. September continued to be a menace; the following year on the same day, September 11th, the second recorded storm hit Louisiana. The intensity and destruction led some to label it a tornado.

Severe storms although the same in devastating destruction and deadly consequences, are called by different titles in different parts of the world.

LOCATION	CALLED
Philippines	Baguio
Indian Ocean	Cyclone
Pacific	Typhoon
Australia	The Willy Willy

ACTIVITY
North Atlantic - Gulf Of Mexico - Caribbean

This area is extremely active because of its warm waters. From 1886 to 1986, 839 tropical storms and hurricanes have been tracked and recorded.

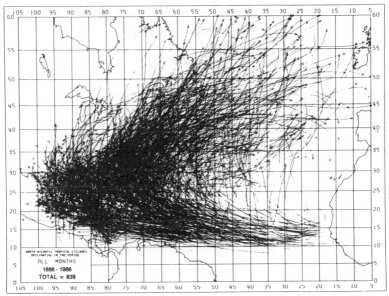

NORTH ATLANTIC - GULF OF MEXICO - CARIBBEAN: THIS AREA IS EXTREMELY ACTIVE BECAUSE OF ITS WARM WATER. FROM 1886 TO 1986, 839 TROPICAL STORMS AND HURRICANES HAVE BEEN TRACKED AND RECORDED ABOVE.

NAMING THE STORMS

In 1950 names were issued to tropical storms and hurricanes for the first time. The first names were selected from the World War II phonetic alphabet consisting of Able, Baker, Charlie, Dog, Easy, etc.

In 1953, feminine names were used for the first time, featuring Alice as the initial feminine name used for a tropical storm (it never reached hurricane force). Barbara was the first feminine-named storm to become a hurricane.

In 1979, masculine names were used for the first time. Masculine and feminine names have been selected alternately since that year; Bob was the first masculine name selected.

Names beginning with the letters Q, U, X, Y and Z are not included because of the scarcity of names beginning with those letters.

HURRICANES CHANGE THEIR NAMES?

When a hurricane or tropical storm moves from the Gulf of Mexico to the Pacific Ocean, it becomes a typhoon and its name is changed.

SEVERE STORMS

Two storms come to the top of the list when making a final decision about the most severe hurricanes to strike Louisiana — the September 29, 1915, hurricane and Betsy, who made her unwelcome visit September 9, 1965.

Hurricane experts report, even though the 1915 storm took 275 lives compared to 75 deaths during Betsy, Betsy was the more severe, having registered higher winds, higher tides and lower minimum pressure. Damage in 1915 amounted to $15,000,000 compared to $1,419,000,000 for Betsy. Even when taking inflation into consideration, Betsy caused considerably greater damage than the 1915 storm.

Destruction of property is devastating, but property (with the exception of personal possessions such as photographs) can be replaced. The greatest loss is human life.

ALL-TIME KILLERS

Thank the good Lord, the #1 storm in terms of lives lost was not in the area of the Gulf of Mexico, but half way around the world. The record goes to Calcutta, India. Calcutta is located in eastern India. The port city is built on low flat swampy delta a few feet above sea level. In 1737, 300,000 people perished because of one storm.

The next deadliest storm stuck eastern Pakistan in 1970, with 200,00 officially dead and 500,000 unofficially dead.

NORTH AMERICA'S NUMBER ONE KILLER STORM

The U.S. weather service representative for the Gulf of Mexico in 1900 was Isaac Monroe Cline. Cline had been in the weather service (started by U.S. Army Signal Corps to predict weather in Gulf of Mexico during war with Mexico) for eighteen years. Eleven of those years were spent in Galveston. Cline, through hard work and unquestionable ability, reference predicting the weather, established a reputation of trust by the people, especially the farm people in the area he served. Someone once jokingly said that when Cline left his home in the morning with an umbrella, everyone carried an umbrella that day. He was, in a sense, a walking weather billboard. Cline thoroughly enjoyed Galveston, as did his wife and three children. The family lived in a two-story house that was specifically designed and built to withstand hurricane winds.

In early September of 1900, a hurricane raised its ugly head north of Cuba. Meteorologist Cline began to collect data and track its progress. He was a master in this field, having collected data from storms around the world, which he studied relentlessly. He collected information, recorded it, and studied it repeatedly. On September 4th and 5th, the storm passed through the Florida straits and headed northwesterly through the Gulf of Mexico. Cline continued to collect data and at this time became very concerned about the storm. He watched and waited for a prediction of its landfall from headquarters of the U.S. Weather Service in Washington, but there was none. Still convinced the storm would make a direct hit on Galveston, he immediately had storm warning flags placed along the coast. His observations on September 8th, at 5:00 a.m. showed the gulf waters coming in over the low parts of the city with the tide

4.5 feet above what the tide should have been. The barometer was falling slowly, the wind was fifteen to seventeen miles per hour from the north, offshore, and the tide was rising with this wind directly against it; such winds under ordinary circumstances caused the tide to fall and give a low tide. The storm swells were increasing in magnitude and frequency and were building up a storm tide, which told him as plainly as though it was a written message that great danger was approaching. Neither the barometer nor the winds were telling him, but the storm tide was telling him to warn the people of the impending danger.

Complete observations describing the weather and unusual tide conditions were telegraphed to the Central Office of the Washington Weather Bureau every two hours from 5:00 a.m. until all the wires went down. Early in the morning of September 8th, Cline could wait no longer for a warning from Washington. Written regulations that were strictly enforced stated that no one except the forecaster in the Central Office of the Weather Bureau at Washington had authority to issue hurricane emergency warnings. Although the forecasters at the central office were kept fully advised, they issued no such warning. Cline had a decision to make — if he gave a warning, which was strictly against the rules, and his prediction did not come to pass, he was subject to being reprimanded, even discharged. On the other hand, if he did not warn his fellow man and the storm came as he predicted, many people would die. Cline had no trouble making the final decision. He harnessed his horse to a two wheel cart, drove along the beaches from one end of the town to the other and warned the people that great danger threatened them. He advised persons from the interior of the state who were summering along the beach to go home immediately. He warned people residing within three blocks of the beach to move to higher portions of the city, that their houses would be undermined by the ebb and flow of the increasing storm tide and possibly could even be washed away. Because of the great respect he commanded from the people,

6000 visitors and residents moved inland and 6000 decided to ride it out. At 3:30 p.m. he had done all he could do in warning the people. His conscience was clear. He then sat down and wrote a message to be sent to the Chief of the Weather Bureau at Washington advising him of the terrible situation. He stated the city was fast going under water and great loss of life would result, and he stressed the need for immediate relief. His assistant had to wade through water up to his waist to get to the telegraph office. Upon arriving, he was advised all telegraph wires were down. He then went to the telephone exchange and found that they had only one wire open to Houston, and it was working only intermittently. The telephone company, sensing the urgency, turned this line over to him with the message going to the Western Union Telegraph office in Houston. Just as this was done, the line went out and Galveston was cut off from all means of communication to the outside world.

Cline walked in water up to his armpits to get to his home. When he got there he found not only his wife and three little girls but fifty other people had taken refuge on the second floor in his home. Included in the fifty were the families of the architect and builder of the structure that was considered hurricane-proof. By 8:30 p.m., the rising water had come close to reaching the second floor. The winds began to blow, and, although the building shook violently, it did hold fast. Then, unfortunately, the unexpected happened. A steel railway about a fourth of a mile long that ran between the home and the Gulf of Mexico was uprooted by the surge of water and like a great ram crashed into the building. The building, with all fifty occupants, was turned over and broken into many pieces. Bodies and debris scattered in all directions. At 11:30 p.m., just three hours after the storm began, the winds died down. Almost everyone in the house, including Cline's wife, had drowned. Luckily, Cline and his three daughters somehow miraculously survived. Sunday, September 9th came with a clear sky, a brilliant sunrise, almost a calm and quiet sea with low tides; a most beautiful day. Many days after the storm had subsided, bodies from the house were still being found. Some washed inland as much as three miles. To illustrate the force of the storm, a three-hundred-foot ocean steamer was torn loose from its mooring and carried several miles inland. A canal had to be dug to get the ship back to deep water.

As Cline later stated, "No written words could describe the horrible conditions that existed in Galveston following the destruction wrought by the storm tide and hurricane winds. No one can explain it, but from recorded time, at times of disaster such as this, ghouls, those who will steal from the dead, began to pounce on dead bodies. Fingers were cut from hands of the dead to get rings. Bodies were found with the heads cutoff so that their necklaces could be taken. Martial law was declared to protect the living and the dead from the ghouls. Large number of responsible citizens were sworn in as guards with instructions to shoot on sight and kill any ghoul seen mutilating the dead. When it was all over, more than 1,000 ghouls were shot before body robbing could be checked."

The dead, when identified, were given proper burials. Almost 2,000 could not be identified, and their bodies were tied to iron rails, placed on barges and hauled out to sea and placed in the briny deep.

In all, 6,000 residents of Galveston lost their lives in this killer storm. Another 6,000 would have perished had it not been for the herculean efforts of Isaac Monroe Cline.

Cline was without question a hero, but at the same time he had to be reprimanded for breaking the rules of the U.S. Weather Service. Chief Willis L. Moore seized the opportunity to slap Cline on the wrist and in doing so help alleviate a sticky situation that existed in Louisiana. Moore, because of the great disaster in Galveston, also realized the need for a forecast district for the gulf states. This would enable quicker response to weather conditions. Moore also used Cline to solve the Louisiana problem. The Times-Democrat, a leading newspaper of New Orleans, ran a daily parallel weather column. On one side ran the weather forecast; the other side gave the actual weather performance of that day. Chief Moore had already tried to persuade the editor to discontinue publishing the controversial column. The editor simply told the inspector that more accurate forecasts would remedy the trouble.

Chief Moore transferred Cline (his slap on the wrist) to New Orleans, Louisiana. The move was made with Cline and his three daughters arriving in New Orleans before anyone in Texas was informed of the transfer. Moore knew of Cline's popularity and the power of the Texas political leaders. Had they known in advance, they could have pooled their political clout and kept Cline in Texas.

Cline's first job upon arriving in New Orleans was to meet with Colonel Page Baker, the able editor of the Times-Democrat. He thanked Baker for the publicity that the newspaper was giving the weather service and hoped that he would continue the column. Cline asked that the weather service be criticized when it failed in its forecast and to be commended when it merited praise. The parallel column of forecast and weather was discontinued shortly after Cline arrived.

In his thirty-five years as chief weather forecaster for Louisiana, Cline's work was not once criticized. In the same period, many accolades were printed emphasizing the value of the forecast of weather, storms and floods.

OUT OF SEASON

Even though hurricane season is June 1 - November 30, four hurricanes have been recorded in May and five in December. The earliest and latest hurricanes on record (using the present classification) were May 16, 1889, and December 30, 1954.

MOST ACTIVE YEAR

1886-1986
1933

(T) TROPICAL STORM: Did Not Reach Hurricane Intensity
(H) HURRICANE: Reached Hurricane Force at Some Point

NO.		DATE	NO.		DATE
1	T	May 14-19	12	H	Aug. 31-Sept. 2
2	H	June 27-July 6	13	H	Sept. 8-21
3	T	July 13-19	14	H	Sept. 10-15
4	T	July 21-27	15	H	Sept. 16-24
5	H	July 26-Aug. 5	16	T	Sept. 27-30
6	T	Aug. 12-20	17	T	Sept. 28-30
7	T	Aug. 16-21	18	H	Oct. 1-9
8	H	Aug. 17-26	19	H	Oct. 25-Nov. 7
9	T	Aug. 24-31	20	T	Oct. 26-30
10	T	Aug. 26-29	21	T	Nov 15-16
11	H	Aug. 28-Sept. 5			

LEAST ACTIVE YEAR

1886-1986
1914

NO.		DATE
1	T	Sept. 14-19

MOST ACTIVE MONTHS

1886-1986

August	184
September	286
October	172

HURRICANE HUNTERS

Army Air Corps Major Joseph P. Duckworth was the first person to deliberately fly an airplane into the eye of a hurricane, on the afternoon of July 27, 1943. He flew his single-engine AT-6 into a hurricane off Galveston twice that day.

SEEDING HURRICANES

The possibility of modifying hurricanes through cloud seeding experiments began in September of 1962. Seeding is a kind of atmospheric judo; since man cannot muster anything approaching the energy of a hurricane, he hopes to use the giant's own energy and size against it.

TORNADOES

When speaking of storms, Louisiana citizens immediately think of hurricanes. One of the main reasons is that, from the time a tropical storm is in the forming stages, the media keeps citizens informed constantly. Sometimes one tropical storm or hurricane can be in the news for several weeks before striking land. Another reason, of course, is that hurricanes do affect a large portion of the area that it strikes. Another good reason, the Gulf of Mexico recorded 839 hurricanes and tropical storms from 1886-1986. When you think of it, that's a lot of media hype time.

On the other hand, did you know, in only 50 years, 1936-1986, 872 tornadoes touched down in the state (not all tropical storms or hurricanes reach land)? This startling statistic shows that far more tornadoes strike Louisiana than hurricanes.

As bad as hurricanes are, most people, I think, would prefer

experiencing a hurricane than a tornado. In a hurricane, many people suffer a little. Tornado victims, although fewer in number, those who are affected usually lose everything.

There is no scientific way of predicting when or where tornadoes will strike as there is for hurricanes. We are given very little warning reference tornadoes, if any. With no media advance notice, tornadoes are not as popular a conversation topic as hurricanes. Chances are, unless tornado experts come up with a plan that allows them to have long-range warnings, it never will be.

LIGHTNING

The one and only good thing about lightning is, if you see it, you do not have to worry about it. Lightning is so fast, if it hits you, you'll never know it.

U.S. records from 1959-1984 show that 2,574 people throughout the United States were struck and killed by

lightning. There were additional people who were struck but survived what would normally be a deadly jolt.

Louisiana in that same 25 year period recorded 97 deaths. June and July, being the most dangerous, accounted for 58% of the total.

Unlike tornadoes, where people are advised in order to protect themselves to lie flat on the ground in a ditch, if you are caught in a level field, and feel your hair stand on end, lightning may be about to strike you. That being the case, you should drop to your knees and bend forward, putting your hands on your knees. Do not lie flat on the ground.

June, July and August are the deadliest months nationwide. Florida is by far the deadliest state to be in, reference lightning. From 1959-1984, Florida recorded 255 deaths, almost 10 percent of the total killed in the U.S. It was also more than twice as many as any other state. Florida, although called the Sunshine State, also holds the record for the most people struck by lightning in one month; 68 people were zapped in the month of July in the same 25 year period.

Maryland reported 81 deaths caused by one bolt of lightning, but this was the result of lightning striking a commercial airplane, resulting in a crash with the loss of 81 lives.

The safest place to be in the United States, if you do not wish to be struck by lightning, is Alaska. In that same 25 year period, they recorded no fatalities.

FLOODS

In the history of Louisiana, as well as the United States, the greatest national disaster was not caused by a hurricane, earthquake or a tornado. The greatest disaster, both in Louisiana and the U.S., happened in 1927 when the mighty Mississippi River and the 250 waterways that empty into its bowels overflowed their banks. Every state (33) on these rivers and bayous was partially under water. In all, 26,000 square miles of land, including farms, towns and cities were flooded. Damage and loss of crops, buildings and lives were horrendous. In addition, seven hundred thousand people were left homeless.

This was not the first time rivers in North America overflowed their banks. But, it was because of the unbelievable devastation of the 1927 flood the federal government finally took the bull by the horns and assumed complete responsibility for flood control of the Mississippi River.

LEVEES

Levee is the French word for raised or elevated. The oldest levee system on record was built along the Nile in Egypt some four thousand years ago. Construction of the oldest levees in North America was started by the French in Louisiana in 1718, the same year the city of New Orleans was founded. The very first priority set by Governor Bienville was to build a levee system to protect the new city from flooding. Engineer LeBlond de la Tour wasted no time building the levee adjacent to the French Quarter. When he completed the job, the levee was three feet high by eighteen feet wide and fifty-four hundred feet long. It was, of course, nothing compared to today's levee system, but it was man's first attempt to harness any river in North America. As more and more people moved into the area to work the fertile land, the levee system was expanded. Those who received land grants adjacent to the river were required to build and maintain a levee the full length of their river front property. By 1733, the levees extended on both the east and west banks, approximately thirty miles above and twelve miles below New Orleans. Unfortunately, that year, the entire levee system was topped, causing extensive flooding on both sides of the river. The levees in some places were so poorly built they washed completely away. This incident was the beginning of the seemingly endless battle of man verses the mighty Mississippi River.

Man was on the losing side for many years. The reason, not all land owners spent the necessary time, energy or money to build and maintain adequate levees. There were no specific guide lines as to how the levees were to be constructed and maintained. The consequence, regular flooding. By 1812, levees extended up river to Baton Rouge on the east bank and about forty miles beyond Baton Rouge on the west bank. By 1849, the levee system in Louisiana reached all the way to the Arkansas border. Unfortunately, the 1849 and 1850 floods once again caused widespread havoc in Louisiana. This calamity led to Congress appropriating fifty thousand dollars for the

United States Army Corps of Engineers to study and survey the
river. The study did go on, but so did flooding. In 1858 and
1859, the river again either breached or topped the poorly-
built levees; and again much of Louisiana's rich soil was
underwater.

With the outbreak of the Civil War in 1861, many years
passed without anything being done to build new levees or
maintain the inadequate levees that were barely standing.
Things got progressively worse when generals on both sides
purposely broke the levees whenever they felt it would help
them militarily. The levee system in Louisiana, or better yet,
what was left of it, went to pot. After the war ended, the carpet
bag government took control of the state. Again many years
passed before anything constructive was done to alleviate the
flooding problem, as this was a low priority under the new
political leaders.

Finally, in 1879, the United States Congress, to renew its
attack on this serious problem, created the Mississippi River
Commission. The MRC in turn called on the United States
Army Corps of Engineers. In 1880, the Corps made what must
have been an eye-opening report, for it resulted in one million
dollars being appropriated to study the problem again. Until
this time, this was the largest dollar investment ever made on

flood control. Would you believe, the money was used not for levee improvements as a means of flood control, but for channel improvement? The result — serious flooding again in 1912 and 1913. You guessed it, this led to further investigation of possible flood control measures. Before anything was done, another serious flood took place in 1916, followed by yet another federal act. While the government was passing acts, the river was doing its act, and that was topping or breaching the levees. The straw that finally broke the camel's back was the 1927 flood. The widespread destruction of this flood led to, as previously pointed out, the Federal Government assuming complete responsibility for flood control of the Mississippi. It was officially called the Flood Control Act of 1928. The United States Army Corps of Engineers was now ready for an all-out effort. After many years, a seemingly impenetrable harness by way of well-built levees was constructed on both banks of the river. Up until now, with very few exceptions, the Corps has had the upper hand. Today there are almost seventeen hundred miles of uniformly built levees on both sides of the Mississippi River that are inspected on a routine basis. A few reach forty or more feet, with the average levee twenty-five feet above the level of the surrounding area. For stability and resistance to water seepage, levees are usually ten times as wide at the base as they are in height.

There were three other important steps taken by the United States Army Corps of Engineers to control the restless River.

1) Floodways to reduce river stages.

2) Improvement and stabilization of channels.

3) Improvement of tributary basins for drainage as well as flood control.

Note:

In major cities, land values along the river are far too valuable to be used for levees. In those cases, concrete flood walls were constructed. They are built with heavily reinforced concrete plus steel sheet piling driven many feet below the ground to prevent seepage.

As the old saying goes, "We've come a long way, baby." From the original three-foot high levee, with no one really in charge, no master plan, no specification or scheduled inspection, to a well-developed plan, highly technical written specifications, with the all important regularly scheduled inspections.

The new system, conceived of, built and maintained by the United States Army Corps of Engineers has weathered with great success the record-setting floods of 1937, 1945, 1950, 1973 and 1975. Presently, the levees are at a height to accommodate and confine river levels eleven to twenty-nine percent greater than the all-time record level reached in 1927. In addition, floodways have been built to reduce the water level if needed.

The mighty river for almost two hundred years had its way. It rambled and roamed where it pleased, when it pleased. Since 1928, man has had the upper hand. Lets hope and pray that man has his way for not only two hundred years, but as the Bible refers to forgiveness, 200 by 200 years.

In 1812, man, through the invention of the powerful steamboat, conquered the swift currents of the mighty

Mississippi River bringing economic prosperity. In 1928, the United States Army Corps of Engineers, through its expertise, put a tight harness on the river, bringing peace of mind and uninterrupted economic prosperity to those who lived along its banks.

RAIN, SNOW & ICE

RAIN

Over the years, Louisiana has been at times extremely wet and at other times uncomfortably dry. For a quick reference, listed below are some all-time Louisiana least and most records.

RAIN

Most - One Year - Statewide
1905 - 75.57 inches average

Least - One Year - Statewide
1889 - 35.83 inches average

Most - One Month - Area
July
1940 - 37.99 inches
Lafayette Parish

City With Most - One Year
1946 - 111.28 inches
Morgan City - St. Mary Parish

Greatest - 24-Hour Period - Area
August 28-29, 1962
22 inches in 24 hours
Sabine National Refuge,
Southwest of Hackberry

IN 119 YEARS, REX (LOUISIANA KING OF MARDI GRAS) CANCELLED PARADE ONLY ONCE FOR RAIN, BUT NOT FOR SNOW?

Since organizing in 1872, the Rex Parade has been cancelled due to rain only once — in 1933.

However, on February 14, 1899, with the coldest temperatures ever recorded in New Orleans, Rex rolled. Along with the all-time low temperature of 6.8 degrees, snow and sleet were also falling.

Approximately one week before Mardi Gras, with each day's temperature breaking previous lows, people started to panic. They were concerned as to whether Rex would cancel his parade. Their anxieties were calmed when Rex put a proclamation in the newspaper several days before Mardi Gras. It stated that the parade would roll as usual, provided the good people cleared the parade route of snow and sleet in front of their homes. The people responded and so did Rex.

AVERAGE ANNUAL PRECIPITATION

YEAR	INCHES	YEAR	INCHES
1931	51.79	1959	58.58
1932	61.85	1960	49.86
1933	56.26	1961	73.10
1934	57.21	1963	42.25
1936	45.40	1964	57.02

YEAR	INCHES	YEAR	INCHES
1937	58.00	1965	46.97
1938	51.71	1966	60.67
1939	51.13	1967	52.02
1940	76.02	1968	58.49
1941	61.15	1969	49.99
1942	57.58	1970	51.25
1943	51.92	1971	52.37
1944	62.28	1972	59.93
1945	62.43	1973	53.45
1946	73.97	1974	63.27
1947	61.12	1975	68.58
1948	54.95	1976	51.28
1949	61.76	1977	59.20
1950	60.76	1978	53.77
1951	48.76	1979	78.54
1952	49.35	1980	57.56
1953	66.21	1981	44.63
1954	43.76	1982	65.35
1955	57.80	1983	67.91
1956	50.64	1984	59.15
1957	67.07	1985	60.45
1958	58.13	1986	53.29

RECORD SNOWFALL

1895 was the only year in recorded history when every parish received snow.

Rayne holds the state record with 24 inches in 1895.

Although Lake Charles received 22 inches in 24 hours (February 14, 1895), no additional snowfall in the city was recorded that year.

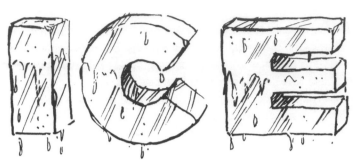

ICE

For an event to out draw a Mardi Gras parade in Louisiana, it has to be something extra spectacular.

Such an event began on Friday, February 17, 1899, and ended four days later. For the first time in recorded history, large ice formations were seen floating down the Mississippi River. These were not small chunks of ice but pieces estimated anywhere from 12 to 24 inches thick and 20 to 100 feet in diameter, with some even larger. The icebergs, with water sprayed from the winds, piled one layer atop another, and formed weird and wonderful shapes that had thousands of Louisianians lining the levee on both sides of the river, saying with excitement in their voices, "Look at that one, no look at that one, wow! Would you look at that one!" A description given by one of the spectators viewing the phenomenon was that it looked like a big field of dirty cotton.

Most steamboat captains feared the consequences of running paddle wheel craft through ice, and tied up their boats until the phenomenon passed. Two excursion boats, the Sunrise and America, with a combined 300 passengers who came to New Orleans for the Mardi Gras, delayed their departures until it was safe.

The skippers of the ferry boats up and down the river, on the other hand, did not discontinue river crossings. On Sunday, February 19, 1899, 8,000 brave New Orleanians threw caution to the winds and took what they knew would be a ride of a lifetime. The ferry captain masterfully maneuvered his small craft cautiously through occasional breaks in the ice. When the boat collided with chunks of ice, the noisy crowd would become as quiet as a church mouse, and once the ice went by, the noise level went back to feverish pitch.

Newspaper accounts were published giving a colorful and chilling description of brave (or stupid) men who literally walked across the Mississippi River in Louisiana by stepping from one large chunk of ice to another until the crossing by foot was achieved.

MISCELLANEOUS

U.S. WEATHER FORECASTING

The U.S. Government's first simultaneous weather report was made from 23 weather stations across the U.S. on November 1, 1870. New Orleans, Louisiana, was one of the original reporting stations.

TV WEATHER FORECASTER WITH A SENSE OF HUMOR

Several years ago, while delivering a talk on meteorology to a civic group, a Louisiana TV weatherman was catching heavy

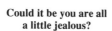
Could it be you are all
a little jealous?

flak from the audience on the accuracy of weather forecasters. He smiled, never losing his composure or his professionalism. When the chastisement subsided, he looked over the audience and said, "I truly love my profession and feel that maybe, some if not all of you are a bit jealous." He paused for a moment and asked the audience, "Who among you has a job where you can be wrong as often as right and still not be fired?" There was a deafening silence and then a resounding round of applause for a man with a tough job who never lost his sense of humor.

Ever since Louisiana was founded in 1682, we have always had a keen interest, almost a passion, for speaking about, reading and listening to weather reports.

WEATHER REPORTS WERE ILLEGAL?

During World War II, it was unlawful to give weather reports over the radio. It was feared that the enemy would use the reports to their benefit.

CONGRESS PASSED LEGISLATION TO SAVE METEOROLOGIST'S JOB?

In 1931, Isaac Monroe Cline, New Orleans' beloved meteorologist, turned 70. Federal Law required government employees to retire at age 70. Louisiana Senator Huey P. Long demanded special legislation to keep him in office. The law was successfully amended to exempt this indispensable man.

UNUSUAL WEATHER FACT

Record temperatures of ninety or more degrees have been recorded in Louisiana during each month of the year.

MONTH	DEGREE	DAY	YEAR	LOCATION
January	92	27	1914	Donaldsonville
February	92	25	1918	Minden
March	95	24	1929	Ruston
April	98	4	1918	Reserve
May	105	30	1911	Abbeville
June	110	20	1936	Dodson
July	111	29	1930	Plain Dealing
August	114	10	1936	Plain Dealing
September	110	1	1951	Lake Providence
October	103	1	1938	Plain Dealing
November	95	10	1915	Robeline
December	90	1	1913	Donaldsonville

WEATHER FORECASTING

Louisianians have always had an interest in and an urge to forecast the weather. Methods of attempting to achieve this are as varied as to how to properly season and boil seafood and the best way to fix bread pudding and red beans and rice. Everyone, it seems, has what he feels is the best method. Some professional weather forecasters have highly sophisticated equipment to help them be as accurate as humanly possible. Others, the average amateur prognosticators, use various but simple equipment. In spite of this, they claim their methods are as accurate as those with the high-tech, state-of-the-art equipment.

One such simple method is as follows:

* Hang a 2" X 6" strip of cloth outside a window.
* Check each morning.
* If it's wet, it's raining.
* If it's stiff, it's freezing.
* If it's white, it's snowing.
* If it's moving, it's windy.
* If it's faded, it's sunny.
* If it's gone, it's a hurricane (or stolen).

CHAPTER 7

LAGNIAPPE

STURDY STOCK THAT HAS TAKEN A LOT

PRIDE IN OUR STATE

LOUISIANIANS — STURDY STOCK THAT HAS TAKEN A LOT

Like the seemingly indestructible cockroach, Louisianians for over 300 years have learned to adapt and survive. They have not only survived, but have prospered where lesser mortals would have thrown in the towel long ago.

Soon after the first settlers built their homes on land that was below sea level, they had an unwelcome visit from the mighty Mississippi River. Until the first levees were built the yearly occasion of flooding lasted not days or even weeks, but months at a time. Shortly after all had suitable housing to live in, many structures were blown to the ground by the first of many hurricanes (1723) that hit the area. Some of the early Indians were about as kind as Mother Nature. They went on a rampage and killed 250 settlers throughout Louisiana. Another of those unwelcome guests were the little critters with the official names, Aedes aegypti, better known as the mosquito. Although small they are deadlier than most snakes. During some yellow fever epidemics, as much as 20 percent of the population died from its deadly sting. Other killers had the ugly names of typhus, cholera and bubonic plague.

The most devastating year for New Orleans, the state's largest city, was 1788. In that one year the city was hard hit by yellow fever, experienced 100 percent flooding, plus a massive fire totally destroyed 856 structures.

The Louisiana Purchase of 1803 was followed in short order by the War of 1812. Louisiana, now part of the United States, was attacked by the greatest military machine in the world. The mighty army of the British empire had just defeated Napoleon's army and was honed to perfection and ready to conquer defenseless little old New Orleans. Not only did Louisiana survive the attack, the mightiest army in the world was literally devastated and torn to shreds.

Between the Battle of New Orleans and the Civil War, Louisiana suffered numerous bank failures that made financial

living seem like walking blindfolded on a tight rope with banana peelings strewn along the way.

New Orleans, although the largest city in the confederacy, and Baton Rouge the capital, both fell early during the Civil War. Once the war had ended the Carpetbag Government made life almost unbearable. Yet, somehow Louisiana's citizens sucked it in and survived.

In spite of hurricanes, floods, fires, yellow fever, military attack, inflation, recession, depression and two World Wars, plus the indignation of 20 years of the Saints football team without a winning season, Louisianians are still around and still adapting to anything and everything that comes their way.

The state's citizens have learned well the lesson whereby they accept every lemon that comes their way. They do not despair, they have learned to squeeze the thing and simply

make lemonade. When they come across a stumbling block, they have learned that by using a positive attitude they can turn it over and make it into a stepping stone. A positive attitude and a good sense of humor are their greatest assets.

With economic conditions as sad as they are in Louisiana today, please keep in mind, economic history proves that every economic bust has been followed by an economic boom.

Yes, Louisianians are like the seemingly indestructible roach; they are sturdy stock that has learned to take a lot and seem always to maintain a good sense of humor.

PRIDE IN OUR STATE

People throughout the United States, no matter where they live, are proud of their hometown, and justifiably so.

The overwhelming majority of Louisiana's citizens are also extremely proud of their state. In spite of poor economic conditions in the 1980s and a shaky start in the 1990s, the vast majority are optimistic, not pessimistic, about the state's future. As one proud Louisianian put it, a pessimist is a man who feels bad when he is feeling good, for fear he'll feel worse if he ever gets to feeling better.

Louisianians are optimistic about the future of their great state. They are as optimistic as the most optimistic man of all times, General George Custer. Yes, Custer was a true optimist. Remember, Custer was surrounded by a thousand Indians on horseback, each with a repeater rifle. Custer, with only six men left, called them to attention. As he looked them over, he noticed one man had an arrow through his arm, and one had lost his rifle. In spite of the overwhelming odds, Custer looked them in the eye, and with great confidence saluted them and said, "Remember, men, during the next charge take no prisoners."